THE
ULTIMATE AUDITION
BOOK

222 Monologues
2 Minutes and Under

Smith and Kraus Monologue Books

If you require prepublication information about upcoming Smith and Kraus books, you may receive our semiannual catalogue, free of charge, by sending your name and address to Smith and Kraus catalogue, PO Box 127, Lyme, NH 03768. Or call us at (800) 895-4331, fax (603) 922-3348.

THE
ULTIMATE
AUDITION BOOK

222
Monologues
2 Minutes and Under

EDITED BY JOCELYN A. BEARD

Monologue Audition Series

SK

A Smith and Kraus Book

A Smith and Kraus Book
Published by Smith and Kraus, Inc.
PO Box 127, Lyme, NH 03768

Copyright ©1997 by Smith and Kraus
All rights reserved
Manufactured in the United States of America

Cover and Text Design by Julia Hill

First Edition: June 1997
10 9 8 7 6 5 4 3

The Library of Congress Cataloging-In-Publication Data
The ultimate audition book: two hundred monologues, two minutes and under / edited by Jocelyn A. Beard. —1st ed.
p. cm. —(Monologue audition series)
Includes bibliographical references.
ISBN 1-57525-066-7
1. Monologues. 2. Acting—Auditions. 3. Drama. I. Beard, Jocelyn. II. Series.
PN2080.U48   1997
808.82'45—dc21   97-10471
CIP

Contents

Women's Monologues

Men's Monologues

15th and 16th Century

17th Century

18th Century

19th Century

20th Century 1950–present

Arden of Feversham

Anonymous
1592

Scene: rural England

Dramatic
Alice: a selfish and manipulating young wife, 18–20

Here, the plotting Alice reveals her desire to see her husband, Arden, dead.

ALICE: Ere noon he means to take horse and away!
Sweet news is this. O that some airy spirit
Would in the shape and likeness of a horse
Gallop with Arden 'cross the Ocean,
And throw him from his back into the waves!
Sweet Mosbie is the man that hath my heart:
And he usurps it, having nought but this,
That I am tied to him by marriage.
Love is a God, and marriage is but words;
And therefore Mosbie's title is the best.
Tush! whether it be or no, he shall be mine,
In spite of him, of Hymen, and of rites.

Arden of Feversham

Anonymous
1592

Scene: rural England

Dramatic
Alice: a selfish and manipulating young wife, 18–20

When Arden chases off the thugs Alice has hired to murder him, the quick-thinking Alice does her best to cover her tracks.

ALICE: Ah, Arden, what folly blinded thee?
Ah, jealous harebrained man, what hast thou done!
When we, to welcome thee with intended sport,
Came lovingly to meet thee on thy way,
Thou drew'st thy sword, enraged with jealousy,
And hurt thy friend whose thoughts were free from harm:
All for a worthless kiss and joining arms,
Both done but merrily to try thy patience.
And me unhappy that devised the jest,
Which, though begun in sport, yet ends in blood! (…)
Could'st thou not see us friendly smile on thee,
When we joined arms, and when I kissed his cheek?
Hast thou not lately found me over-kind?
Did'st thou not hear me cry "they murder thee"?
Called I not help to set my husband free?
No, ears and all were witched; ah me accursed
To link in liking with a frantic man!
Henceforth I'll be thy slave, no more thy wife,
For with that name I never shall content thee.
If I be merry, thou straightways thinks me light;
If sad, thou sayest the sullens trouble me;
If well attired, thou thinks I will be gadding;
If homely, I seem sluttish in thine eye:
Thus am I still, and shall be while I die.
Poor wench abused by thy misgovernment!

Friar Bacon and Friar Bungay

Robert Greene
Circa 1589

Scene: England under the reign of Henry III

Serio-Comic
Margaret: the keeper's daughter

When a young man courts her at the Harleston Fair,
Margaret wonders at his refined speech and manner.

MARGARET: *(Aside.)* How different is this farmer from the rest
That erst as yet have pleased my wandering sight!
His courtesy gentle, smelling of the court;
Facile and debonair in all his deeds;
Proportioned as was Paris, when, in gray,
He courted Œnon in the vale by Troy.
Great lords have come and pleaded for my love;
Who but the Keeper's lass of Fressingfield?
And yet methinks this farmer's jolly son
Passeth the proudest that hath pleased mine eye.
But, Peg, disclose not that thou art in love
And show as yet no sign of love to him,
Although thou well wouldst wish him for thy love;
Keep that to thee till time doth serve thy turn,
To show the grief wherein thy heart doth burn.

Friar Bacon and Friar Bungay

Robert Greene

Circa 1589

Scene: England under the reign of Henry III

Dramatic
Margaret: the keeper's daughter

Here, Margaret prepares to enter a convent.

MARGARET: Ah, father, when the harmony of heaven
Soundeth the measures of a lively faith,
The vain illusions of this flattering world
Seem odious to the thoughts of Margaret.
I loved once,—Lord Lacy was my love,
And now I hate myself for that I loved,
And doted more on him than on my God,
For this I scourge myself with sharp repents.
But now the touch of such aspiring sins
Tells me all love is lust but love of heavens;
That beauty used for love is vanity.
The world contains naught but alluring baits,
Pride, flattery, and inconstant thoughts.
To shun the pricks of death, I leave the world,
And vow to meditate on heavenly bliss,
To live in Framlingham a holy nun,
Holy and pure in conscience and in deed;
And for to wish all maids to learn of me
To seek heaven's joy before earth's vanity. (…)
Now farewell world, the engine of all woe!
Farewell to friends and father! Welcome Christ!
Adieu to dainty robes! This base attire
Better befits an humble mind to God
Than all the show of rich habiliments.
Farewell, O love! and, with fond love, farewell
Sweet Lacy, whom I loved once so dear!
Ever be well, but never in my thoughts,
Lest I offend to think on Lacy's love:
But even to that, as to the rest, farewell!

The Resurrection

The York Pageant of the Carpenters
Circa 1450

Scene: the empty tomb

Dramatic
Mary of Magdala: one of Christ's followers, 20s

Here, Mary laments the death of the man she loved.

MARY: Alas, what shall now worth on me?
    My caitiff heart will break in three
    When I think on that body free,
    How it was spilt:
    Both feet and hands nailed till a tree,
    Withouten guilt.
    Withouten guilt the true was ta'en,
    For trepass did he never none:
    The woulds he suffered many one
    Were for my miss;
    It was my deed he was for slain,
    And nothing his.
    How might I, but I loved that sweet—
    That for my love tholed wounds wet,
    And sithen be graven under the greet—
    Such kindness kithe?
    There is nothing to that we meet
    May make me blithe.

A Chaste Maid in Cheapside
Thomas Middleton
Circa 1613

Scene: England

Serio-Comic
Maudlin: a goldsmith's wife, 30–40

Here, the ambitious Maudlin nags her daughter, Moll, for not trying hard enough to find a husband.

MAUDLIN: Have you played over all your old lessons o'the virginals? (…) Yes, you are a dull maid alate, methinks you had need have somewhat to quicken your green sickness; do you weep? A husband. Had not such a piece of flesh been ordained, what had us wives been good for? To make salads, or else cried up and down for samphire. To see the difference of these seasons! When I was of your youth, I was lightsome, and quick, two years before I was married. You fit for a knight's bed—drowsy browed, dull eyed, drossy sprited—I hold my life you have forgot your dancing: when was the dancer with you? (…)
Last week? When I was of your bord, he missed me not a night, I was kept at it; I took delight to learn, and he to teach me, pretty brown gentleman, he took pleasure in my company; but you are dull, nothing comes nimbly from you, you dance like a plumber's daughter, and deserve two thousand pounds in lead to your marriage, and not in goldsmith's ware.

All for Love; or the World Well Lost

John Dryden
1677

Scene: Alexandria, 30 BC

Dramatic
Octavia: wife of Marc Antony and sister of Caesar, 30s

Octavia has followed her husband to Alexandria with the intent of winning him back from Cleopatra. Here, she offers to save Antony from her brother's wrath.

OCTAVIA: My hard fortune
  Subjects me still to your unkind mistakes.
  But the conditions I have brought are such
  You need not blush to take: I love your honor,
  Because 'tis mine; it never shall be said,
  Octavia's husband was her brother's slave.
  Sir, you are free—free, ev'n from her you loathe;
  For, though my brother bargains for your love,
  Makes me the price and cément of your peace,
  I have a soul like yours; I cannot take
  Your love as alms, nor beg what I deserve.
  I'll tell my brother we are reconciled;
  He shall draw back his troops, and you shall march
  To rule the East: I may be dropped at Athens;
  No matter where, I never will complain,
  But only keep the barren name of wife,
  And rid you of the trouble.

All for Love; or the World Well Lost

John Dryden
1677

Scene: Alexandria, 30 BC

Dramatic
Cleopatra: Queen of Egypt, 30s

Following the suicide of her lover, Marc Antony, the passionate Queen prepares to join him in death. Here, she presents her arm to the asp and suffers its fatal bite.

CLEOPATRA: 'Tis sweet to die when they would force life on me,
  To rush into the dark abode of death,
  And seize him first. If he be like my love,
  He is not frightful, sure.
  We're now alone, in secrecy and silence;
  And is not this like lovers? I may kiss
  These pale, cold lips; Octavia does not see me,
  And, oh, 'tis better far to have him thus
  Than see him in her arms. —Oh, welcome, welcome! (...)
  Short ceremony, friends;
  But yet it must be decent. First, this laurel
  Shall crown my hero's head; he fell not basely,
  Nor left his shield behind him. Only thou
  Couldst triumph o'er thyself, and thou alone
  Wert worthy so to triumph. (...)
  Dull that thou art! Why, 'tis to meet my love
  As when I saw him first, on Cydnus' bank,
  All sparkling, like a goddess. So adorn'd
  I'll find him once again; my second spousals
  Shall match my first in glory. Haste, haste, both,
  And dress the bride of Antony.
  Now seat me by my lord. I claim this place,
  For I must conquer Caesar too, like him,
  And win my share o'the world. Hail, you dear relics
  Of my immortal love!

Oh, let no impious hand remove you hence,
But rest forever here! Let Egypt give
His death that peace which it denied his life.
Reach me the casket. (…)
Welcome, thou kind deceiver!
Thou best of thieves, who, with an easy key,
Dost open life, and, unperceiv'd by us,
Ev'n steal us from ourselves, discharging so
Death's dreadful office better than himself,
Touching our limbs so gently into slumber
That Death stands by, deceiv'd by his own image,
And thinks himself but sleep. (…)
He comes too late t'invade the rights of death.
Haste, bare my arm, and rouse the serpent's fury.
Coward flesh,
Wouldst thou conspire with Caesar to betray me,
As thou wert none of mine? I'll force thee t'it,
And not be sent by him,
But bring, myself, my soul to Antony. *(Turns aside and then shows her arm bloody)*
Take hance; the work is done (…)
Already, death, I feel thee in my veins.
I go with such a will to find my lord
That we shall quickly meet.
A heavy numbness creeps through every limb,
And now 'tis at my head; my eyelids fall
And my dear love is vanish'd in a mist.
Where shall I find him, where? Oh, turn me to him,
And lay me on his breast! —Caesar, thy worst;
Now part us if thou canst.

Epicoene
Ben Jonson
1609

Scene: London

Serio-Comic
Mistress Otter: a nagging wife, 30–40

Mistress Otter seems to relish the constant upbraiding of her subservient husband, as the following harangue illustrates.

MISTRESS OTTER: By my integrity, I'll send you over to the Bankside, I'll commit you to the Master of the Garden, if I hear but a syllable more. Must my house or my roof be polluted with the scent of bears and bulls, when it is perfumed for great ladies? Is this according to the instrument, when I married you? that I would be princess, and reign in mine own house; and you would be my subject, and obey me? What did you bring me, should make you thus peremptory? Do I allow you your half-crown a day, to spend where you will, among your gamesters, to vex and torment me at such times as these? Who gives you your maintenance, I pray you? Who allows you your horse-meat and man's-meat? your three suits of apparel a year? your four pair of stockings, one silk, three worsted? your clean linen, your bands and cuffs, when I can get you to wear 'em? 'Tis mar'l you have 'em on now. Who graces you with courtiers or great personages, to speak to you out of their coaches and come home to your house? Were you ever so much as looked upon by a lord or a lady before I married you, but on the Easter or Whitsun-holidays? and then out at the Banqueting House window, when Ned Whiting or George Stone were at the stake. (…) Answer me to that. And did not I take you up from thence, in an old, greasy buff doublet, with points, and green velvet sleeves out at the elbows? You forget this.

The Innocent Mistress

Mary Pix
1697

Scene: London

Dramatic
Bellinda: a woman who mistakenly believes the man she
loves to be married to another, 20s

Here, sad Bellinda bemoans her loveless fate.

BELLINDA: Honour and love. Oh, the torture to think they are domestic foes that must destroy the heart that harbours 'em. Had my glass but been my idol, my mind loose, unconstant, wavering, like my sex, then I might have 'scaped these pangs. Love, as passing meteors, with several fires just warms their breasts and vanishes, leaving no killing pain behind. 'Tis only foolish. I have made a god of my desire greater than ever the poets feigned. My eyes received no pleasure but what his sight gave me. No music charmed my ears but his dear voice. Racks, gibbets and dungeons, can they equal losing all my soul admires? Why named I them? Can there be greater racks
Than what despairing, parting lovers find,
To part, when both are true, both would be kind?

The Lady of Pleasure

James Shirley
1635

Scene: London

Serio-Comic
Celestina: an extravagant widow, 20–30

When her household steward tries to warn Celestina that she is developing a questionable reputation for her excesses, she angrily scolds him.

CELESTINA: Make you my governor; audacious varlet,
How dare you interpose your doting counsel?
Mind your affairs with more obedience,
Or I shall ease you of an office, sir.
Must I be limited to please your honour,
Or for the vulgar breath confine my pleasures?
I will pursue 'em in what shapes I fancy:
Here, and abroad, my entertainments shall
Be oftener and more rich. Who shall control me?
I live i'th' Strand, whither few ladies come
To live and purchase more than fame. I will
Be hospitable, then, and spare no cost
That may engage all generous report
To trumpet forth my bounty and my bravery
Till the court envy and remove. I'll have
My house the academy of wits, who shall
Exalt it with rich sack and sturgeon,
Write panegyrics of my feasts, and praise
The method of my witty superfluities;
The horses shall be taught, with frequent waiting
Upon my gates, to stop in their career
Toward Charing Cross, spite of the coachman's fury,
And not a tilter but shall strike his plume
When he sails by my window; my balcony
Shall be the courtier's idol, and more gazed at
Than all the pageantry at Temple Bar
By country clients.

The Learned Women

Moliere
1672

Scene: Paris

Dramatic
Armande: a foolish young woman who fancies herself a
philosopher, 20s

*Armande has put off Clitandre's proposal of marriage for two
years in hopes that the young man's physical passion will evolve
into something more spiritual. When the greatly frustrated
Clitandre finally proposes to Armande's younger sister, Armande
furiously demands that he account for his inability to express "perfect love."*

ARMANDE: Do I oppose the wishes of your heart
When I seek to root out their vulgar part,
And ask a purity in your desires
Consistent with what perfect love requires?
You couldn't school your thoughts to abstinence,
For me, from the degrading claims of sense?
And you've no taste for the serene delight
Felt when two disembodied hearts unite?
You can live only in this brutish wise?
Only with all the train of fleshly ties?
And to nourish the fires produced in you
You must have marriage, and what follows too?
Oh, what a strange love! Hear me, if you please:
Noble souls burn with no such flames as these!
In all their glow the senses have no part,
And all they seek to marry is the heart;
With scorn they leave aside other desires.
Their flames are pure, like the celestial fires.
Their love gives vent only to virtuous sighs,
And crass desires they utterly despise.
Nothing impure contaminates their goals;
They love for love alone, a love of souls;
Their transports are directed to the mind;
The body is ignored and left behind.

The Plain Dealer
William Wycherley
1676

Scene: London

Dramatic
Fidella: a woman pining for the love of a man who loves another, 20s

Fidella loves Manly, and masquerading as a man, has fol-lowed him to sea. Now returned to London, Manly pursues Olivia. Here, the heartbroken Fidella muses on the time she has wasted.

FIDELLA: His Olivia, indeed, his happy Olivia!
    Yet she was left behind, when I was with him:
    But she was ne'er out of his mind or heart.
    She has told him she loved him; I have showed it,
    And durst not tell him so, till I had done,
    Under this habit, such convincing acts
    Of loving friendship for him, that through it
    He first might find out both my sex and love;
    And, when I'd had him from his fair Olivia,
    And this bright world of artful beauties here,
    Might then have hoped, he would have looked on me,
    Amongst the sooty Indians; and I could
    To choose there live his wife, where wives are forced
    To live no longer, when their husbands die;
    Nay, what's yet worse, to share 'em; whilst they live
    With many rival wives. But here he comes,
    And I must yet keep out of his sight, not
    To lose it forever.

The Rival Queens

Nathaniel Lee
1677

Scene: Babylon

Dramatic
Roxana: wife of Alexander the Great, 20s

When Alexander takes the beautiful Statira as his second wife, passionate Roxana flies into a rage. Here, she threatens to ruin their honeymoon night.

ROXANA: When you retire to your romantic cell,
    I'll make thy solitary mansion hell;
    Thou shalt not rest by day, nor sleep by night,
    But still Roxana shall thy spirit fright.
    Wanton, in dreams, if thou dar'st dream of bliss,
    Thy roving ghost may think to steal a kiss;
    But when to his sought bed thy wand'ring air
    Shall, for the happiness it wished, repair,
    How will it groan to find thy rival there!
    How ghastly wilt thou look when thou shalt see,
    Through the drawn curtains, that great man and me,
    Wearied with laughing joys, shot to the soul,
    While thou shalt grinning stand, and gnash thy teeth, and howl.
    (…)
    The king and I in various pictures drawn,
    Clasping each other, shaded o'er with lawn,
    Shall be the daily presents I will send
    To help thy sorrow to her journey's end.
    And when we hear at last thy hour draws nigh,
    My Alexander, my dear love, and I
    Will come and hasten on thy ling'ring fates,
    And smile and kiss thy soul out through the grates.

The Royal Mischief

Mary Delarivier Manley
1696

Scene: the Castle of Phasia in Libardian

Dramatic
Bassima: a woman married to a man she doesn't love, 20s

*Bassima was married to Levan Dadiare for political reasons,
but her heart belongs to Osman, the Chief Visier. Here, the
wretched Bassima reveals her illicit feelings to Osman.*

BASSIMA: You, only you.
　　The Earth's united hatred could not harm
　　Me equal to your kindness. It strikes at
　　Innocence and fame, and lays my virtue
　　Level with the vilest,
　　Makes marriage an uneasy bondage,
　　And the embraces of my lord a loathsome
　　Penance. What would you more? The time is come
　　That I must speak to make my ruin certain.
　　Like some prophetic priestess, full of the
　　God that rends her, must breathe the baleful
　　Oracle or burst. My crowding stars just
　　Now appear to fight, and dart upon me
　　With malignant influence. Nor can my
　　Reason stop the dictates of my heart,
　　They echo from my mouth in sounds of love,
　　But such a love as never woman knew.
　　'Twas surely given by fate, I would have said
　　From Heaven, but that inspires but good,
　　And this is surely none.

The Royal Mischief

Mary Delarivier Manley
1696

Scene: the Castle of Phasia in Libardian

Dramatic
Bassima: a woman married to a man she doesn't love, 20s

Here, Bassima pleads with Osman to never see her again.

BASSIMA: You like a lover entertain your fancy,
    But I have still the fatal land in view,
    Where death of honour waits on that of life.
    Now let us part, lest we should meet on that.
    See, at your feet I beg for life and fame.
    Nay, do not interrupt me, I'll not rise.
    Could I have found relief from Heaven, or hence,
    (Pointing to her breast.) I had not kneeled to you.
    My inauspicious fate comes fast upon me.
    You, only you, can stop its headlong course.
    I charge you then, by honour, glory, fame,
    By love, the mighty god that now torments me,
    You yield me not, a sinful slave, to death,
    Torn in my conscience, mangled in my virtue,
    But fly from hence, never to see me more.
    Or should you stay, dare not to meet my eyes
    With yours, those tell-tales of your passion,
    Lest I break rudely from my husband's arms,
    And fly to death in yours.

Sir Patient Fancy

Aphra Behn
1678

Scene: London

Serio-Comic
Lady Knowell: an affected learned woman, 40–60

Here, the well-read Lady Knowell sings the praises of reading the classics in their original languages.

LADY KNOWELL: Ay, Mr. Fancy, in consultation with the ancients.—Oh, the delight of books! when I was of their age, I always employed my looser hours in reading—if serious, 'twas Tacitus, Seneca, Plutarch's *Morals,* or some such useful author; if in an humor gay, I was for poetry, Virgil, Homer, or Tasso. Oh, that love between Rinaldo and Armida, Mr. Fancy! Ah, the caresses that fair Corcereis gave, and received from the young warrior; ah, how soft, delicate, and tender! Upon my honor, I cannot read them in the excellence of their original language, without I know not what emotions. (...)

Oh, faugh, Mr. Fancy, what have you said, mother tongue! Can any thing that's great or moving be expressed in filthy English?—I'll give you an energetical proof, Mr. Fancy; observe but divine Homer in the Grecian language—*Ton d'apamibominous prosiphe podas ochus Achilleus!* Ah, how it sounds! which English'd dwindles into the most grating stuff:—Then the swift-foot Achilles made reply. Oh, faugh.

Tartuffe

Moliere
1644

Scene: 17th century Paris

Dramatic
Mariane: a young woman betrothed to a man she despises,
18–20

*Mariane's father, Orgon, has been conned by the swindling
Tartuffe into offering the scoundrel his lovely young daughter in marriage. Here, poor Mariane begs her father to
allow her to enter a convent rather than marry a man she
doesn't love.*

MARIANE: *(Falling to her knees.)*
Sir, by that Heaven which sees me here distressed,
And by whatever else can move your breast,
Do not employ a father's power, I pray you,
To crush my heart and force it to obey you,
Nor by your harsh commands oppress me so
That I'll begrudge the duty which I owe—
And do not so embitter and enslave me
That I shall hate the very life you gave me.
If my sweet hopes must perish, if you refuse
To give me to the one I've dared to choose,
Spare me at least—I beg you, I implore—
The pain of wedding one whom I abhor;
And do not, by a heartless use of force,
Drive me to contemplate some desperate course. (…)
I don't resent your love for him. Allow
Your heart free rein, Sir; give him your property,
And if that's not enough, take mine from me;
He's welcome to my money; take it, do,
But don't, I pray, include my person too.
Spare me, I beg you; and let me end the tale
Of my sad days behind a convent veil.

The Tragedy of Sophonisba

John Marston
1606

Scene: Libya, the second Punic War

Dramatic
Erictho: a witch, 30–40

Erictho has tricked the mighty Syphax into believing that he has made love to Sophonisba when in fact it was the old crone herself in his bed. When the King discovers that he has been with the witch, she laughs at his outrage.

ERICTHO: Why, fool of kings, could thy weak soul imagine
　　　That 'tis within the grasp of heaven or hell
　　　To enforce love? Why know, love dotes the Fates;
　　　Jove groans beneath his weight. More ignorant thing,
　　　Know we, Erictho, with a thirsty womb,
　　　Have coveted full threescore suns for blood of kings.
　　　We that can make enraged Neptune toss
　　　His huge curled locks without one breath of wind;
　　　We that can make heaven slide from Atlas' shoulder;
　　　We, in the pride and height of covetous lust,
　　　Have wished with woman's greediness to fill
　　　Our longing arms with Syphax' well-strung limbs.
　　　And dost thou think, if philters or hell's charms
　　　Could have enforced thy use, we would have damned
　　　Brain-sleights? No, no. Now are we full
　　　Of our dear wishes. Thy proud heat well wasted
　　　Hath made our limbs grow young. Our love, farewell,
　　　Know he that would force love, thus seeks his hell.

The Tragedy of Sophonisba

John Marston
1606

Scene: Libya, the second Punic War

Dramatic
Sophonisba: a woman who has sacrificed her life for her city, 20s

Sophonisba has given herself to Syphax to save her beloved Carthage from ruin by his armies. When her rightful husband, Massinissa, defeats Syphax in battle and confronts her, Sophonisba begs him to let her die a free woman.

SOPHONISBA: Whate'er man thou art,
  Of Libya thy fair arms speak. Give heart
  To amazed weakness; hear her, that for long time
  Hath seen no wished light. Sophonisba,
  A name for misery much known, 'tis she
  Entreats of thy graced sword this only boon:
  Let me not kneel to Rome, for though no cause
  Of mine deserves their hate, though Massinissa
  Be ours to heart, yet Roman generals
  Make proud their triumphs with whatever captives.
  O 'tis a nation which from soul I fear,
  As one well knowing the much-grounded hate
  They bear to Asdrubal and Carthage blood.
  Therefore with tears that wash thy feet, with hands
  Unused to beg, I clasp thy manly knees.
  O save me from their fetters and contempt,
  Their proud insults and more than insolence!
  Or, if it rest not in thy grace of breath
  To grant such freedom, give me long-wished death;
  For 'tis not much loathed life that now we crave,
  Only an unshamed death and silent grave
  We will now deign to bend for.

Venice Preserved; or, A Plot Discovered

Thomas Otway

1682

Scene: Venice

Dramatic
Belvidera: a young woman in love, 20s

Belvidera has married Jaffeir, with whom she is deeply in love. Here, she greets her new husband with great affection.

BELVIDERA: If love be treasure, we'll be wondrous rich:
    I have so much, my heart will surely break with't.
    Vows cannot express it: when I would declare
    How great's my joy, I am dumb with the big thought:
    I swell and sigh, and labor with my longing.
    Oh, lead me to some desert wide and wild,
    Barren as our misfortunes, where my soul
    May have its vent; where I may tell aloud
    To the high heavens an every list'ning planet,
    With what a boundless stock my bosom's fraught;
    Where I may throw my eager arms about thee,
    Give loose to love with kisses, kindling joy,
    And let off all the fire that's in my heart.

Volpone

Ben Jonson
1606

Scene: Venice

Dramatic
Celia: a young woman trying to save her virtue, 20s

*Celia's husband, Corvino, has offered her favors to the
unscrupulous Volpone in a misguided attempt to become
the wealthy nobleman's sole heir. Here, the terrified Celia
begs Volpone to either let her go or kill her.*

CELIA: If you have ears that will be pierced; or eyes
    That can be opened; a heart may be touched;
    Or any part that yet sounds man about you;
    If you have touch of holy saints, or heaven,
    Do me the grace to let me 'scape. If not,
    Be bountiful and kill me. You do know,
    I am a creature, hither ill betrayed,
    By one, whose shame I would forget it were.
    If you will deign me neither of these graces,
    Yet feed your wrath, sir, rather than your lust
    (It is a vice comes nearer manliness),
    And punish that unhappy crime of nature,
    Which you miscall my beauty; flay my face,
    Or poison it with ointments, for seducing
    Your blood to this rebellion. Rub these hands,
    With what may cause an eating leprosy,
    E'en to my bones and marrow: any thing,
    That may disfavor me, save in my honor—
    And I will kneel to you, pray for you, pay down
    A thousand hourly vows, sir, for your health;
    Report, and think your virtuous—

The Witch of Edmonton

William Rowley, Thomas Dekker, John Ford
1628

Scene: England

Dramatic
Elizabeth Sawyer: a witch, 40–60

Here, a woman branded by all as a witch indulges in a bit of self-pity.

ELIZABETH SAWYER: And why on me? Why should the envious world
    Throw all their scandalous malice upon me?
    'Cause I am poor, deformed and ignorant,
    And like a bow buckled and bent together
    By some more strong in mischiefs than myself,
    Must I for that be made a common sink
    For all the filth and rubbish of men's tongues
    To fall and run into? Some call me witch,
    And, being ignorant of myself, they go
    About to teach me how to be one, urging
    That my bad tongue, by their bad usage made so,
    Forspeaks their cattle, doth bewitch their corn,
    Themselves, their servants and their babes at nurse. (...)
    This they enforce upon me, and in part
    Make me to credit it.

The Witch of Edmonton

William Rowley, Thomas Dekker, John Ford
1628

Scene: England

Dramatic
Elizabeth Sawyer: a witch, 40–60

*When Elizabeth is accused of being a witch, she angrily
confronts her accusers with the following insight.*

ELIZABETH SAWYER: A witch! Who is not?
Hold not that universal name in scorn then.
What are your painted things in princes' courts,
Upon whose eyelids lust sits, blowing fires
To burn men's souls in sensual hot desires,
Upon whose naked paps a lecher's thought
Acts sin in fouler shapes than can be wrought? (…)
No, but far worse.
These by enchantments can whole lordships change
To trunks of rich attire, turn ploughs and teams
To Flanders mares and coaches, and huge trains
Of servitors to a French butterfly.
Have you not city-witches who can turn
Their husband's wares, whole standing shops of wares,
To sumptuous tables, gardens of stol'n sin;
In one year wasting what scare twenty win?
Are not these witches? (…)
Why then on me
Or any lean old beldam? Reverence once
Had wont to wait on age. Now an old woman
Ill-favoured grown with years, if she be poor
Must be called bawd or witch. Such so abused
Are the coarse witches, t'other are the fine,
Spun for the devil's own wearing.

The Beggar's Opera
John Gay
1728

Scene: London

Serio-Comic
Mrs. Peachum: a woman of questionable morality, 40s

The Peachums are delighted when their daughter, Polly, catches the eye of the notorious Macheath, who is prepared to pay handsomely for her favors. When Polly announces that she and the highwayman have been married, her mother chides the girl for her foolishness.

MRS. PEACHUM: You baggage, you hussy! you inconsiderate jade! had you been hanged, it would not have vexed me, for that might have been your misfortune; but to do such a mad thing by choice!—The wench is married, husband. (…)
I knew she was always a proud slut; and now the wench hath played the fool and married, because forsooth she would do like the gentry. Can you support the expense of a husband, hussy, in gaming, drinking and whoring? have you money enough to carry on the daily quarrels of man and wife about who shall squander most? There are not many husbands and wives who can bear the charges of plaguing one another in a handsome way. If you must be married, could you introduce nobody into our family but a highwayman? Why, thou foolish jade, thou wilt be as ill used, and as much neglected, as if thou hadst married a lord!

The Careless Husband
Colley Cibber
1705

Scene: Windsor

Serio-Comic
Lady Easy: long-suffering wife, 20–30

Lady Easy's wayward husband is making her crazy, as the following diatribe illustrates.

LADY EASY: Was ever woman's spirit, by an injurious husband, broke like mine? A vile, licentious man! must he bring home his follies too? Wrong me with my very servant! Oh, how tedious a relief is patience! and yet in my condition 'tis the only remedy, for to reproach him with my wrongs is taking on myself the means of a redress, bidding defiance to his falsehood, and naturally but provokes him to undo me. Th'uneasy thought of my continual jealousy may tease him to a fixed aversion, and hitherto, though he neglects, I cannot think he hates me.—It must be so, since I want power to please him, he never shall upbraid me with an attempt of making him uneasy. My eyes and tongue shall yet be blind and silent to my wrongs, nor would I have him think my virtue could suspect him, till by some gross, apparent proof of his misdoing he forces me to see—and to forgive it.

The Careless Husband

Colley Cibber

1705

Scene: Windsor

Serio-Comic
Lady Betty Modish: a vain and shallow woman, 20–30

When Lady Betty is cautioned by a friend that the married man she has been having an affair with will tell all his friends about her intimate charms, the foolish homewrecker ignores the advice.

LADY BETTY MODISH: Pshaw! Will anything a man says make a woman less agreeable? Will his talking spoil one's complexion, or put one's hair out of order? And for reputation—look you, my dear, take it for a rule that as amongst the lower rank of people no woman wants beauty that has fortune, so amongst people of fortune no woman wants virtue that has beauty. But an estate and beauty joined is of an unlimited—nay, a power pontifical, makes one not only absolute, but infallible. A fine woman's never in the wrong, or if we were, 'tis not the strength of a poor creature's reason that can unfetter him. Oh, how I love to hear a wretch curse himself for loving on, or now and then coming out with a
Yet, for the plague of human race,
This devil has an angel's face.

The Castle Spectre

Matthew G. Lewis
1797

Scene: a castle

Dramatic
Angela: a young woman being held prisoner, 20s

The evil Osmond has taken Angela captive. Here, the anxious young woman waits to be rescued by the man she loves.

ANGELA: Will it never arrive, this tedious lingering hour? Sure an age must have elapsed since the Friar left me, and still the bell strikes not one!—"Percy, does thy impatience equal mine? Dost thou too count the moments which divide us?—Dost thou too chide the slowness of Time's pinions, which moved so swiftly when we strayed together on the Cheviot Hills?—Methinks I see him now, as he paces the Conway's margin: If a leaf falls, if a bird flutters, he flies towards it, for he thinks 'tis the foot-step of Angela: Then, with slow steps and bending head, disappointed he regains the fisher's cottage. Perhaps, at this moment, his eyes like mine are fixed on yonder planet; perhaps, this sweet wind which plays on my cheek, is freighted with the sighs of my Lover.—Oh! sigh no more, my Percy!—Soon shall I repose in safety on your bosom; soon again see the moon shed her silver light on Cheviot, and hear its green hills repeat the carol of your mellow horn!"

Douglas
John Home
1757

Scene: a castle in the west of Scotland, 12th century

Dramatic
Lady Randolph: a melancholy widow, 30–40

When her new husband prepares to leave for war against Danish invaders, Lady Randolph is reminded of the bloody Scottish and English wars that took the life of Douglas, her beloved first husband.

LADY RANDOLPH: War I detest: but war with foreign foes,
　　Whose manners, language, and whose looks are strange,
　　Is not so horrid, nor to me so hateful,
　　As that which with our neighbors oft we wage.
　　A river here, there an ideal line,
　　By fancy drawn, divides the sister kingdoms.
　　On each side dwells a people similar,
　　As twins are to each other; valiant both;
　　Both for their valor famous through the world.
　　Yet will they not unite their kindred arms,
　　And, if they must have war, wage distant war,
　　But with each other fight in cruel conflict.
　　Gallant in strife, and noble in their ire,
　　The battle is their pastime. They go forth
　　Gay in the morning, as to summer sport;
　　When ev'ning comes, the glory of the morn,
　　The youthful warrior, is a clod of clay.
　　Thus fall the prime of either hapless land;
　　And such the fruit of Scotch and English wars.

Fatal Curiosity

George Lillo
1736

Scene: Penryn in Cornwall

Dramatic
Charlot: a young woman grieving for the man she loved,
20s

*When a stranger accuses Charlot of being unfaithful to
Wilmot while he was missing at sea, she hotly protests her
love.*

CHARLOT: 'Tis enough!
Detested falsehood now has done its worst.
And art thou dead? And would'st thou die, my Wilmot,
For one thou thought'st unjust? Thou soul of truth!
What must be done? Which way shall I express
Unutterable woe? Or how convince
Thy dear, departed spirit of the love,
Th'eternal love, and never-failing faith
Of thy much-injured, lost, despairing Charlot? (...)
If, as some teach, the mind intuitive,
Free from the narrow bounds and slavish ties
Of sordid earth that circumscribe its power
While it remains below, roving at large,
Can trace us to our most concealed retreat,
See all we act, and read our very thoughts,
To thee, O Wilmot, kneeling I appeal!
If e'er I swerved in action, word, or thought
From the serverest constancy and truth,
Or ever wished to taste a joy on earth
That centered not in thee, since last we parted,
May we ne'er meet again but thy loud wrongs
So close the ear of Mercy to my cries
That I may never see those bright abodes
Where truth and virtue only have admission,
And thou inhabit'st now.

Fatal Curiosity

George Lillo

1736

Scene: Penryn in Cornwall

Dramatic
Agnes: a woman driven to commit murder by poverty,
50–60

*The family fortune gone and their son lost at sea, Agnes
and her husband are tempted to kill a mysterious stranger
for money. When her husband balks at committing such a
desperate crime, Agnes angrily blames his excesses for their
shameful state.*

AGNES: Barbarous man!
   Whose wasteful riots ruined our estate
   And drove our son, ere the first down had spread
   His rosy cheeks, spite of my sad presages,
   Earnest entreaties, agonies, and tears,
   To seek his bread 'mongst strangers, and to perish
   In some remote, inhospitable land?
   The loveliest youth, in person and in mind,
   That ever crowned a groaning mother's pains!
   Where was thy pity, where thy patience then?
   Thou cruel husband! Thou unnat'ral father!
   Thou most remorseless, most ungrateful man!
   To waste my fortune, rob me of my son,
   To drive me to despair, and then reproach me
   For being what thou'st made me!

The Jealous Wife

George Colman
1761

Scene: London

Serio-Comic
Lady Freelove: a scheming woman, 30–40

Lady Freelove has used the innocent young Harriet as a pawn in her idle affairs d'cour. When Harriet's father accuses Lady Freelove of having brought about Harriet's ruination, the manipulating society matron protests her innocence.

LADY FREELOVE: Mercy on me! how boisterous are these country gentlemen! Why really, Mr. Russet, you rave like a man in Bedlam; I'm afraid you'll beat me: and then you swear most abominably! How can you be so vulgar? I see the meaning of this low malice: but the reputations of women of quality are not so easily impeached; my rank places me above the scandal of little people, and I shall meet such petty insolence with the greatest ease and tranquillity. But you and your simple girl will be the sufferers: I had some thoughts of introducing her into the first company; but now, madam, I shall neither receive nor return your visits, and will entirely withdraw my protection from the ordinary part of the family.

Know Your Own Mind

Arthur Murphy
1777

Scene: London

Serio-Comic
Lady Bell: a duplicitous young woman, 20s

*Here, Lady Bell describes the enjoyment she takes from tor-
turing the men who court her.*

LADY BELL: I do so. I mean to be married, and am frank enough to
own it. But you may let 'concealment feed on your damask
cheek'. My damask cheek, I hope, was made for other purposes. (...)
Not in the least; a natural character. One would not, to be sure,
tell a hideous man that one loves him, but, when one has
encouraged him by degrees and drawn him on, like a new
glove, and perhaps done him a mischief in the doing it, why
then one would draw him off again, and maybe ask a pretty fellow to help a body; and then the wretch looks so piteous and
kneels at your feet!—Then rises in a jealous fit—'I take my lasting farewell! never to return—no, never! What! to her? who
encouraged me?—encouraged him? who primised?—broke her
promise? The treacherous, faithless, dear deluding'—Then
returns in an instant, hands dangling—eyes imploring—tongue
faltering—'Lady Bell,—Lady Bell,—when you know that I adore
you!' And I burst out into a fit of laughter in his face. Oh, that's
my joy, my triumph, my supreme delight!

The London Merchant; or The History of George Barnwell

George Lillo
1731

Scene: London

Dramatic
Millwood: an evil scheming woman, 30s

Millwood has deliberately seduced young George Barnwell in order to ruin the innocent youth by forcing him to perform criminal acts such as theft and murder. When she is discovered and apprehended, she vehemently declares her hatred of men.

MILLWOOD: Men of all degrees and all professions I have known, yet found no difference but in their several capacities; all were alike wicked to the utmost of their power. In pride, contention, avarice, cruelty and revenge, the reverend priesthood were my unerring guides. From suburb-magistrates, who live by ruined reputations, as the inhospitable natives of Cornwall do by shipwrecks, I learned that to charge my innocent neighbors with my crimes, was to merit their protection; for to screen the guilty is the less scandalous when many are suspected, and detraction, like darkness and death, blackens all objects and levels all distinction. Such are your venal magistrates, who favor none but such as, by their office, they are sworn to punish. With them, not to be guilty is the worst of crimes, and large fees privately paid are every needful virtue. (…)
I know you and I hate you all. I expect no mercy and I ask for none; I followed my inclinations, and that the best of you do every day. All actions seem alike natural and indifferent to man and beast, who devour, or are devoured, as they meet with others weaker or stronger than themselves.

The London Merchant; or The History of George Barnwell

George Lillo
1731

Scene: London

Dramatic
Maria: a young woman saying good-bye to the man she loves, 20s

Maria's fiancee, George, has been led astray by the evil Millwood, for whom he has committed murder. Here Maria visits the man who betrayed her love just before he is led off to the gallows.

MARIA: Yes, fruitless is my love, and unavailing all my sighs and tears. Can they save thee from approaching death—from such a death? Oh, terrible idea! What is her misery and distress, who sees the first, last object of her love, for whom alone she'd live—for whom she'd die a thousand, thousand deaths, if it were possible—expiring in her arms? Yet she is happy when compared to me. Were millions of worlds mine, I'd gladly give them in exchange for her condition. The most consummate woe is light to mine. The last of curses to other miserable maids is all I ask for relief, and that's denied me. (...)
All but this; his dreadful catastrophe, virtue herself abhors. To give a holiday to suburb slaves, and passing entertain the savage herd who, elbowing each other for a sight, pursue and press upon him like his fate! A mind with piety and resolution armed may smile on death. But public ignominy, everlasting shame,—shame, the death of souls—to die a thousand times, and yet survive even death itself, in never-dying infamy—is this to be endured? Can I, who live in him, and must, each hour of my devoted life, feel all these woes renewed—can I endure this?

The Lying Valet

David Garrick

1741

Scene: London

Serio-Comic
Kitty: an insightful ladies' maid, 20s

When her mistress falls in love with the penniless Gayless,
Kitty laments the blinding property of love.

KITTY: O woman, woman, foolish woman! she'll certainly have this
Gayless: nay, were she as well convinced of his poverty as I am,
she'd have him. A strong dose of love is worse than one of
ratafia; when it once gets into our heads, it trips up our heels,
and then good night to discretion. Here is she going to throw
away fifteen thousand pounds; upon what? faith, little better
than nothing—he's a man, and that's all—and heaven knows
mere man is but small consolation.
Be this advice pursued by each fond maid,
Ne'er slight the substance for an empty shade:
Rich, weighty sparks alone should please and charm ye:
For should spouse cool, his gold will always warm ye.

The Rivals
Richard Brinsley Sheridan
1775

Scene: Bath

Dramatic
Julia: a young woman terminating her engagement, 20s

*Julia has been pushed to the limit by her fiancee's constant
questioning of her loyalty and love for him. Here, she finally
declares that their engagement has ended.*

JULIA: Yet hear me—My father loved you, Faulkland! and you preserved the life that tender parent gave me; in his presence I
pledged my hand—*joyfully* pledged it—where before I had
given my heart. When, soon after, I lost that parent, it seemed
to me that Providence had, in Faulkland, shown me whither to
transfer without a pause my grateful duty, as well as my affection: hence I have been content to bear from you what pride
and delicacy would have forbid me from another.—I will not
upbraid you by repeating how you have trifled with my sincerity.— (...)
After such a year of trial—I might have flattered myself that I
should not have been insulted with a new probation of my sincerity, as cruel as unnecessary! A trick of such a nature as to
show me plainly that when I thought you loved me best, you
even then regarded me as a mean dissembler; an artful, prudent
hypocrite. (...)
I now see it is not in your nature to be content or confident in
love. With this conviction—I never will be yours. While I had
hopes that my persevering attention and unreproaching kindness might in time reform your temper, I should have been
happy to have gained a dearer influence over you; but I will not
furnish you with a licensed power to keep alive an incorrigible
fault, at the expense of one who never would contend with
you. (...)
But one word more.—As my faith has once been given to you, I
never will barter it with another.—I shall pray for your happiness
with the truest sincerity; and the dearest blessing I can ask of

heaven to send you will be to charm you from that unhappy temper which alone has prevented the performance of our solemn engagement.—All I request of *you* is that you will yourself reflect upon this infirmity, and when you number up the many true delights it has deprived you of—let it not be your *least* regret that it lost you the love of one—who would have followed you in beggary through the world!

Slaves in Algiers; or, Struggle for Freedom

Susanna Haswell Rowson
1794

Scene: Algiers

Dramatic
Rebecca: a woman held captive, 30s

Rebecca and her son, Augustus, have been taken captive in Algiers. Rebecca's unscrupulous master has recently sold Augustus to another household. Here, unhappy Rebecca worries about her son.

REBECCA: *(Discovered reading.)* "The soul, secure in its existence, smiles
At the drawn dagger, and defies its point.
The stars shall fade away, the sun itself
Grow dim with age, and nature sink in years,
But thou shall flourish in immortal youth,
Unhurt, amidst the war of elements,
The wreck of matter, or the crush of worlds." *(Lays down the book.)*
Oh, blessed hope! I feel within myself that spark of intellectual heavenly fire that bids me soar above this mortal world, and all its pains or pleasures—its pleasures! Oh, long—long since I have been dead to all that bear the name! In early youth, torn from the husband of my heart's selection—the first, only object of my love. Bereft of friends, cast on an unfeeling world, with only one, poor stay on which to rest the hope of future joy. I have a son—my child! My dear Augustus, where are you now? In slavery. Grant me patience, heaven! Must a boy born in Columbia, claiming liberty as his birthright, pass all his days in slavery? How often have I gazed upon his face, and fancied I could trace his father's features; how often have I listened to his voice, and thought his father's spirit spoke within him. Oh, my adored boy! Must I no more behold his eyes beaming with youthful ardor when I have told him how his brave countrymen purchased their freedom with their blood? Alas! I see him now but seldom. And when we meet, to think that we are slaves—poor, wretched slaves, each serving different masters—my eyes overflow with tears. I have but time to protect his life, and at some future day restore his liberty.

Three Weeks After A Marriage

Arthur Murphy
1776

Scene: London

Serio-Comic
Lady Racket: a woman returned home from a gaming party,
20–30

Here, Lady Racket entertains her husband by recounting her evening playing cards.

LADY RACKET: Ah, you fond fool!—But I hate gaming. It almost meta-morphoses a woman into a fury. Do you know that I was frighted at myself several times tonight? I had a huge oath at the very tip of my tongue. (…)
I caught myself at it, but I bit my lips and so I did not disgrace myself. And then I was crammed up in a corner of the room with such a strange party at a whist-table, looking at black and red spots. Did you mind them? (…)
There was that strange unaccountable woman, Mrs. Nightshade. She behaved so strangely to her husband, a poor, inoffensive, good-natured, good sort of a good-for-nothing kind of man; but she so teased him—'How could you play that card? Ah, you have a head and so has a pin! You are a numskull, you know you are—Madam, he has the poorest head in the world, he does not know what he is about—you know you don't—Ah, fie! I am ashamed of you!' (…)
And then, to crown all, there was my Lady Clackit, who runs on with an eternal larum of nothing, out of all season, time and place. In the very midst of the game, she begins—'Lard, me'm, I was apprehensive I should not be able to wait on your lady-ship—my poor little dog, Pompey—the sweetest thing in the world—spade led!—there's the knave—I was fetching a walk, me'm, the other morning in the Park; a fine frosty morning it was; I love frosty weather of all things. Let me look at the last trick—and so, me'm, little Pompey—Oh! if your la'yship was to see the dear little creature pinched with the frost, and mincing

his steps along the Mall, with his pretty little innocent face—I vow I don't know what to play—and so, me'm, while I was talking to Captain Flimsey—Your la'yship knows Captain Flimsey?—Nothing but rubbish in my hand—I can't help it—and so, me'm, five odious frights of dogs beset my poor little Pompey—the dear creature has the heart of a lion, but who can resist five at once? And so Pompey barked for assistance. The hurt he received was upon his chest. The doctor would not advise him to venture out till the wound was healed for fear of inflammation—Pray what's trumps?'

The Tragedy of Jane Shore

Nicholas Rowe

1714

Scene: London, June 1483

Dramatic
Alicia: a woman of dark passion, 20s

Alicia has sacrificed her virtue and her birthright to Lord Hastings. When he no longer desires her, Alicia angrily accuses him of treason of the heart.

ALICIA: O thou false lord!
    I would be mistress of my heaving heart,
    Stifle this rising rage, and learn from thee
    To dress my face in easy, dull indifference.
    But 'two'not be; my wrongs will tear this way,
    And rush at once upon thee. (…)
    O thou cool traitor! thou insulting tyrant!
    Dost thou behold my poor distracted heart,
    Thus rent with agonizing love and rage,
    And ask me what it means? Art thou not false?
    Am I not scorned, forsaken, and abandoned—
    Left, like a common wretch, to shame and infamy;
    Giv'n up to be the sport of villains' tongues,
    Of laughing parasites, and lewd buffoons;
    And all because my soul has doted on thee
    With love, with truth, and tenderness unutterable?

The Way of the World

William Congreve
1700

Scene: London

Serio-Comic
Lady Wishfort: a woman deceived, 30–40

Waitwell, a serving man and husband to Foible, has masqueraded as "Sir Rowland" in a scheme to distract Lady Wishfort from her obsession with Edward Mirabell, Waitwell's employer. When Lady Wishfort discovers that she has been made the butt of this cruel joke, she lashes out at Foible.

LADY WISHFORT: Out of my house, out of my house, thou viper, thou serpent, that I have fostered! thou bosom traitress, that I raised from nothing!—begone, begone, begone, go, go!—that I took from washing of old gauze and weaving of dead hair, with a bleak blue nose, over a chafing-dish of starved embers, and dining behind a traverse rag, in a shop no bigger than a birdcage,—go, go, starve again, do, do! (…)
Away, out, out, go set up for yourself again!—do, drive a trade, do, with your three-penny worth of small ware, flaunting upon a pack-thread, under a brandy-seller's bulk, or against a dead wall by a ballad-monger! Go, hang out an old Frisoneer gorget, with a yard of yellow colberteen again! do! an old gnawed mask, two rows of pins, and a child's fiddle; a glass necklace with the beads broken, and a quilted nightcap with one ear! Go, go, drive a trade!—These were your commodities, you treacherous trull, this was your merchandise you dealt in, when I took you into my house, placed you next myself, and made you governante of my whole family! You have forgot this, have you, now you have feathered your nest?

The West Indian

Richard Cumberland
1771

Scene: London

Serio-Comic
Louisa: a young woman in love 18–20

*Louisa has been advised by her brother to stop thinking
about Belcour, the man with whom she has fallen in love.
Here, smitten Louisa questions the practicality of her brother's suggestion.*

LOUISA: Think of him no more! Well, I'll obey; but if a wand'ring
uninvited thought should creep by chance into my bosom, must
I not give the harmless wretch a shelter? Oh! yes; the great atri-
ficer of the human heart knows every thread he wove into its
fabric, nor puts his work to harder uses than it was made to
bear: my wishes then, my guiltless ones, I mean, are free. How
fast they spring within me at that sentence! Down, down, ye
busy creatures! Whither would you carry me? Ah! there is one
amongst you, a forward, new intruder, that, in the likeness of
an offending, generous man, grows into favor with my heart.
Fie, fie upon it! Belcour pursues, insults me: yet such is the
fatality of my condition, that what should rouse resentment,
only calls up love.

Altorf

Frances Wright
1819

Scene: Switzerland

Dramatic
Rosina: a young woman in love with a married man, 18–20

Rosina has just discovered that the man she loves is married. Here, she bemoans her unhappy fate.

ROSINA: I am the first, who should not be at all.
And why not be? I come to seek the man
Who rules my destiny, who hath my faith,
My thoughts, my love, my soul, my all in keeping;
And do I wrong to seek the face of such?
I know not; but this world hath strange opinions,
And very wondrous creeds of right and wrong.
If with our little lips we speak an oath
That men do register, albeit the heart
Cries out aloud and damns the sounding falsehood,
'Tis still a saintly seal, and passeth current
In earth and heaven. But when two pure hearts
Seek testimony at the ear of God,
And have the record of their true affections,
Here is no saintly bond, no gordion knot
But what the sword of law may cleave asunder.
Poor, trusting, simple Rosa! Oh, ye young hearts,
Who come confiding on this slippery world,
That I could teach you but my piteous tale
And save you from my very cruel heartache!
Would I had never come! And do I wish it?
I wish I do not. No, I'll see him yet!
See him once more—gaze once, but once again
Upon that worshipped face—Ha! Is that he
Upon you hilltop, marked against the sky?
Forbid it; heaven! A woman! Then, his wife.
He stoops—he kisses her—he waves his hand!

Oh, traitor! Traitor! Traitor! I will away.
I'll fly—I have not strength. Oh, I have heard on't—
Heard of jealousy: its sting, its venomed tooth—
I've heard on't oft. I never thought to feel it.

Arms and the Man

George Bernard Shaw
1894

Scene: Bulgaria, 1885

Dramatic
Louka: an ambitious and passionate servant, 18–20

*Louka secretly loves Sergius, a young military hero recently
returned from battle. When Sergius complains of the lack
of bravery in the ranks he commands, Louka speaks with
passion on what she would do with her life, if only she
were allowed.*

LOUKA: How easy it is to talk! Men never seem to me to grow up:
they all have schoolboy's ideas. You don't know what true
courage is. (…)
Look at me! how much am I allowed to have my own will? I
have to get your room ready for you: to sweep and dust, to
fetch and carry. How could that degrade e if it did not degrade
you to have it done for you? But *(With subdued passion.)* if I
were Empress of Russia, above everyone in the world, then!! Ah
then, though according to you I could shew no courage at all,
you should see, you should see. (…)
I would marry the man I loved, which no other queen in Europe
has the courage to do. If I loved you, though you would be as
far beneath me as I am beneath you, I would dare to be the
equal of my inferior. Would you dare as much if you loved me?
No: if you felt the beginnings of love for me you would not let
it grow. You would not dare: you would marry a rich man's
daughter because you would be afraid of what other people
would say of you.

The Bear

Anton Chekhov, Trans. by Carol Rocamora
1888

Scene: the drawing room of Popova's country estate, somewhere in provincial Russia

Comedic
Helen Popov: a pretty young widow; 20s–30s

*A young widow confronts her belligerent neighbor, who is
demanding collection of a debt owed by her late husband,
and who starts spouting philosophy about men and women
in love.*

HELEN POPOV: A man! *(With a malicious laugh.)* A man, faithful and
true in love! What a laugh! *(Passionately.)* Really, how can you
possibly say such a thing? Faithful and true, my foot! Now that
we're on the subject, then let me inform you, for your information, that of all the men I've ever known or shall know, the
noblest among them was my late husband...I loved him passionately, with all of my being, as only a young and intelligent
woman *can* love; I gave him my youth, my happiness, my life,
my fortune, I lived and breathed for him, I worshipped the
ground he walked on, like a heathen...and what happened?
This noblest of men has shamelessly betrayed me at every
opportunity! After his death I found drawers full of love letters
in his desk, and while he was alive—I shudder to think of it—he
would leave me alone for weeks at a time, he would chase
other woman right under my nose, he was unfaithful to me, he
squandered my money, he laughed at my feelings...And in spite
of it all, I loved him and remained true to him...And what's
more, he died, and still I remain faithful and true to him. I've
buried myself forever between these four walls, I shall wear
these widow's weeds to my grave...

Bertram; or, The Castle of St. Aldobrand

Charles Robert Maturin
1816

Scene: Sicily, 11th century

Dramatic
Imogine: a woman married to a man she does not love,
20–30

Believing her beloved Bertram to be dead, Imogine marries St. Aldobrand to save her father from ruin. Here, the lonely wife sits in her apartment and dwells with melancholy upon her fate.

IMOGINE: Yes,
    The limner's art may trace the absent feature,
    And give the eye of distant weeping faith
    To view the form of its idolatry;
    But oh! the scenes 'mid which they met and parted—
    The thoughts, the recollections sweet and bitter—
    Th' Elysian dreams of lovers, when they loved—
    Who shall restore them?
    "Less lovely are the fugitive clouds of eve,
    "And not more vanishing"—if thou couldst speak,
    Dumb witness of the secret soul of Imogine,
    Thou might'st acquit the faith of womankind—
    Since thou wast on my midnight pillow laid
    Friend hath forsaken friend—the brotherly tie
    Been lightly loosed—the parted coldly met—
    Yea, mothers have with desperate hands wrought harm
    To little lives from their own bosoms lent.
    But woman still hath loved—if that indeed
    Woman e'er loved like me.

The Colleen Brawn

Dion Boucicault
1860

Scene: Ireland

Dramatic
Mrs. Cregan: a nagging mother, 40–50

*When her son announces that he plans to marry a woman
of whom Mrs. Cregan does not approve, she offers the lad
the following admonishment.*

MRS. CREGAN: Hardress—I speak not for myself, but for you—and I
would rather see you in your coffin than married to this poor,
lowborn, silly, vulgar creature. I know, my son, you will be miserable, when the infatuation of first love is past; when you turn
from her and face the world, as one day you must do, you will
blush to say, 'This is my wife.' Every word from her mouth will
be a pang to your pride—you will follow her movements with
terror—the contempt and derision she excites will rouse you
first to remorse, and then to hatred—and from the bed to
which you go with a blessing, you will rise with a curse.

The Colleen Brawn

Dion Boucicault
1860

Scene: Ireland

Dramatic
Sheelah: a superstitious woman, 40–50

A young woman has been found drowned in a nearby stream. Here, Sheelah tells the tale to her feverish son.

SHEELAH: The poor Colleen! Oh, yo, Danny, I knew she'd die of the love that was chokin' her. He didn't know how tindher she was, when he give her the hard word. What was that message the masther sent to her, that ye wouldn't let me hear? It was cruel, Danny, for it broke her heart entirely; she went away that night, and, two days after, a cloak was found floatin' in the reeds, under Brikeen Bridge; nobody knew it but me. I turned away, and never said—. The crature is drowned, Danny, and wo to them as dhruve her to it. She has no father, no mother to put a curse on him, but there's the Father above that niver spakes till the last day, and then—*(She turns and sees Danny gasping, his eyes fixes on her, supporting himself on his arm.)* Danny! Danny! he's dyin'—he's dyin'!

A Doll's House

Ibsen, Trans. by Brian Johnston and Rick Davis
1879

Scene: Norway

Dramatic
Nora: a woman preparing to leave her husband, 28–30

After eight years of marriage, Nora has finally realized that her life has never been her own. Here, she confronts her husband just before leaving him.

NORA: *(Shaking her head.)* You've never loved me. You just thought it was a lot of fun to be in love with me. (…) It's a fact, Torvald. When I was at home with Papa, he told me all his opinions; so of course I had the same opinions. And if I had any others, I kept them hidden, because he wouldn't have liked that. He called me his doll-child, and he played with me like I played with my dolls. Then I came to your house— (…) *(Undisturbed.)* I mean, I went from Papa's hands into yours. You set up everything according to your taste; so of course I had the same taste, or I pretended to, I'm not really sure. I think it was half-and-half, one as much as the other. Now that I look back on it, I can see that I've lived like a beggar in this house, from hand to mouth; I've lived by doing tricks for you, Torvald. But that's how you wanted it. You and Papa have committed a great sin against me. It's your fault that I've become what I am.

Ernest Maltravers

Louisa Medina

1838

Scene: a garden by Lake Como, Italy

Serio-Comic
Lady Florence: a young woman in love, 18–20

*Here, Lady Florence confesses her love for Lumley Ferrers to
the trees and flowers of her garden.*

LADY FLORENCE: Oh, woman, woman! Man's choicest blessing and his
slave! The sport of feeling and the puppet of fortune—how
hard a lot is thine! Like the modest violet, panting for the shade
thou livest to pour thy odors on the lowly valley; yet when
transplanted to the hotbeds of pride, the hand that tore thee
from thy native home rejects and scorns thee! Well, I never felt
more in a humor to moralize in all my life. I am condemned
without judge or jury. Let me see: yon beautiful sycamore will
do for the Council of Ten. So, "Oh, yes! Come into court,
Florence Saxingham, Lady of Touwood Lee, and answer to the
charge of love!" Mercy, what a crime! "Guilty or not guilty of
love for Ernest Maltravers?" Oh, not guilty, my lords and gentlemen—not guilty! "And to a second charge: guilty or not guilty
of love for Lumley Ferrers?" Oh, guilty! Very guilty, my lords,
but recommended to mercy. *(Enter Ernest, behind.)* For pray
consider, what can a poor woman do but fall in love with goodness, courage, and kindness? So in love I am, and pray, my lord,
forgive Florence Saxingham; she'll never do so any more.

The Family Legend

Joanna Baillie
1810

Scene: the Isle of Mull

Dramatic
Helen: a woman used as a political pawn, 20s

*To end war between the Campbells and the MacLeans,
Helen has married a MacLean, and in so doing, loses De
Gray, the man she has always loved. Here, she tries to say
farewell to De Gray, who has risked his life to visit her in
the MacLean castle.*

HELEN: O go not from me with that mournful look!
    Alas! thy generous heart, depressed and sunk,
    Looks on my state too sadly.—
    I am not, as thou thinkst, a thing so lost
    In woe and wretchedness.—Believe not so!
    All whom misfortune with her rudest blasts
    Hath buffeted, to gloomy wretchedness
    Are not therefore abandoned. Many souls
    From cloistered cells, from hermits' caves, from holds
    Of lonely banishment, and from the dark
    And dreary prison-house, do raise their thoughts
    With humble cheerfulness to heaven, and feel
    A hallowed quiet, almost akin to joy;
    And may not I, by heaven's kind mercy aided,
    Weak as I am, with some good courage bear
    What is appointed for me?—O be cheered!
    And let not sad and mournful thoughts of me
    Depress thee thus.—When thou art far away,
    Thou'lt hear, the while, that in my father's house
    I spend my peaceful days, and let it cheer thee.
    I too shall every southern stranger question,
    Whom chance may to these regions bring, and learn
    Thy fame and prosperous state.

The Female Enthusiast

Sarah Pogson
1807

Scene: France during the Revolution

Dramatic
Charlotte Corday: French patriot who stabbed Marat to death in his bath, 20–30

Though sympathetic to the Revolution, Charlotte is horrified by the violence of the Reign of Terror and so murders the evil Marat. Here, Charlotte awaits her execution in prison.

CHARLOTTE CORDAY: While the soul ranges through the boundless scope
    Of never dying thought, and views at ease
    Each object cherished by its mortal ties,
    What are the body's bonds? Mere spider threads.
    Yet when we long to clasp a father's hand;
    To meet a brother's eye, a friend's caress;
    To hear the accents of the voice we love—
    How strains the eye, how bends the listening ear!
    The arms extend—but ah, extend in vain!
    The visions fade, and the sick heart is void. (Pauses.)
    In blest reality we yet shall meet!
    Oh, may my tongue defend its noble cause,
    Convincing, with triumphant energy,
    That vice should be destroyed and virtue live—
    That he has perished who was most its foe,
    And justly fell a victim at its shrine.

The Forest Princess; or, Two Centuries Ago

Charlotte Mary Sanford Barnes
1844

Scene: The banks of the Powhatan River in the land of
Pawhatan named Virginia by Sir Walter Raleigh, 1609

Dramatic
Pocahontas: the Forest Princess, daughter of Powhatan,
18–20

*When Pocahontas is taken prisoner by Ratcliffe and his
men, she angrily confronts those who conspire against her
father.*

POCAHONTAS: In a daughter's ear,
    Who dare to breathe that word against her sire?
    To free his country from invader's tread,
    He tries the arts his rugged life has taught.
    Ye blame the red man, yet adopt his wiles.
    Why do ye practice treachery, deceit,
    Trampling on hospitable gratitude
    By thus constraining me? Oh, shame! The stream
    Of patriot love flows in *my father's* heart,
    Though shadowed so by dark, enlacing woods,
    The sun of mercy cannot always pierce
    Their thick unwholesome gloom. No such excuse
    Is *yours;* for from the current of your souls
    The tomahawk of ages has hewn down
    All that impeded the pure light of heaven!

Ghosts

Ibsen, Trans. by Brian Johnston and Rick Davis
1881

Scene: a country estate in West Norway

Dramatic
Helene Alving: a woman haunted by her past, 40s

When she is accused by her pastor of being a bad mother for sending her son, Osvald, away to be raised by strangers, Helene reveals that her late husband was an abusive alcoholic whose profligate lifestyle led to his early demise. She sent her son away to save him from his father's evil influence.

HELENE ALVING: I've had to endure a lot in this house. To keep him home evenings—and nights—I had to hoin him over a bottle up in his room. I had to sit alone with him, toasting and drinking with him, listening to his obscene, nonsensical talk, had to drag him into bed with my bare hands— (…)
I endured it for my little boy. But when that last humiliation occurred—my own maid—then I swore to myself that this would be the end! And so I took power in this house—absolute power over him and everything else. Now I had a weapon against him, you see; he didn't dare object. Then I sent Osvald away. he was almost seven—he'd begun to notice things, and ask questions the way children do. And I couldn't bare that, Manders. I thought the child would be poisoned just by breathing the air in this polluted house. And now you can see why he never set foot here as long as his father lived. No one can possibly know what that has cost me.

Ghosts

Ibsen, Trans. by Brian Johnston and Rick Davis
1881

Scene: a country estate in West Norway

Dramatic
Helene Alving: a woman haunted by her past, 40s

*Helen's inability to escape the memories of her unhappy
past is here evidenced in her speculation that ghosts—not
only of people, but also of ideas—are everywhere, making
progress to a better life impossible.*

HELENE ALVING: Let me tell you what I mean by that. I'm terrified—and
it's made me something of a coward—because my mind is
haunted by the dead among us, and I'm afraid I can never be
completely free from them. (…)
The dead among us—ghosts. When I heard Regina and Osvald
in there, I saw ghosts. I almost believe we are ghosts, all of us.
It's not just what we inherit from our fathers and mothers that
walks again in us—it's all sorts of dead old ideas and dead
beliefs and things like that. They don't exactly *live* in us, but
there they sit all the same and we can't get rid of them. All I
have to do is pick up a newspaper, and I see ghosts lurking
between the lines. I think there are ghosts everywhere you turn
in this country—as many as there are grains of sand—and then
there we all are, so abysmally afraid of the light.

The Great Galeoto

Jose Echegaray, Trans. by Hannah Lynch
1881

Scene: Madrid

Dramatic
Teodora: a young woman wrongly accused of infidelity, 20s

*When her sister-in-law informs her that her husband has
been fatally wounded in a duel fought to preserve her
honor, Teodora passionately defends her love and loyalty.*

TEODORA: I hear you, but while I listen, it seems no longer a sister, a
friend, a mother that speaks to me, so hateful are your words.
Your lips seem to speak at inspiration of the devil's prompting.
Why should you strive to convince me that little by little I am
ceasing to love my husband, and that more and more I am
imbued with an impure tenderness, with a feeling that burns
and stains? I who love Julian as dearly as ever, who would give
the last drop of blood in my body for a single breath of life for
him—for him, from whom I am now separated *(Points to his
room.)* —why, should I like to go in there this moment, if your
husband did not bar my way, and press Julian once more in my
arms. I would so inundate him with my tears, and so close him
round with the passion of my love, that its warmth would melt
his doubts, and his soul would respond to the fervor of mine.
But it is not because I adore my husband that I am bound to
abhor the faithful and generous friend who so nobly risked his
life for me. And if I don't hate him, is that a reason to conclude
that I love him? The world can think such things. I hear such
strange stories, and such sad events have happened, and calum-
ny has so embittered me, that I find myself wondering if public
opinion can be true—in doubt of myself. Can it be that I really
am the victim of a hideous passion, unconsciously influenced by
it? and in some sad and weak moment shall I yield to the senses, and be subjugated by this tyrannous fire?

John Gabriel Borkman

Ibsen, Trans. by Rolf Fjelde
1896

Scene: Norway

Dramatic
Ella Rentheim: a woman seeking to punish the man who
broke her heart, 30–40

*Years ago, Borkman abandoned his love for Ella in order to
advance his career. Here, she angrily confronts him with his
crime of the heart.*

ELLA RENTHEIM: *(Advancing on him.)* You're a murderer! You've committed the supreme, mortal sin! (…)
You've killed the capacity to love in me. *(Approaching him.)* Can
you understand what that means? In the Bible it speaks of a
mysterious sin for which there *is* no forgiveness. I've never
known before what that could be. Now I know. The great
unforgivable sin is—to murder the love in a human being. (…)
You've done that. I've never truly realized before this evening
exactly what it was that happened to me. That you abandoned
me and turned instead to Gunhild—I took that as no more than
a simple lack of constancy on your part, and the result of heartless calculation on hers. I almost think I despised you a little—in
spite of everything. But *now* I see it! You abandoned the
woman you *loved!* Me, me, me! The dearest that you had in
this world you were ready to sign away for profit. It's a double
murder you're guilt of! Murder of your own soul, and of mine!

Lady Windermere's Fan

Oscar Wilde
1892

Scene: London

Serio-Comic
The Duchess of Berwick: a society matron, 40–50

Here, the pragmatic Duchess offers the following assess-
ment of the character of men to Lady Windermere, whose
husband has recently strayed.

DUCHESS OF BERWICK: Oh, all of them, my dear, all of them, without
exception. And they never grow any better. Men become old,
but they never become good. (…)
[Yes, we begin like that.] It was only Berwick's brutal and inces-
sant threats of suicide that made me accept him at all, and
before the year was out he was running after all kinds of petti-
coats, every color, every shape, every material. In fact, before
the honeymoon was over, I caught him winking at my maid, a
most pretty, respectable girl. I dismissed her at once without a
character.—No, I remember I passed her on to my sister; poor
dear Sir George is so short-sighted, I thought it wouldn't matter.
But it did, though it was most unfortunate. *(Rises.)* And now,
my dear child, I must go, as we are dining out. And mind you
don't take this little aberration of Windermere's too much to
heart. Just take him abroad, and he'll come back to you all
right. (…)
Yes, dear, these wicked women get our husbands away from us,
but they always come back, slightly damaged, of course. And
don't make scenes, men hate them!

Masks and Faces

Charles Reade
1852

Scene: London

Dramatic
Mabel Vane: a young woman whose husband has deceived her, 22

Mabel has traveled to London to surprise her husband, Ernest. When she arrives, she discovers that Ernest has been having an affair with an actress. Here, the distraught Mabel imagines what she would say to her rival should they ever meet.

MABEL VANE: Oh, that she were here, as this wonderful portrait is; and then how I would plead to her for my husband's heart! *(She addresses the supposed picture.)* Oh, give him back to me! what is one more heart to you? you are so rich, and I am so poor, that without his love I have nothing; but must sit me down and cry till my heart breaks—give him back to me, beautiful, terrible woman; for with all your gifts you cannot love him as his poor Mabel does. Oh, give him back to me—and I will love you and kiss your feet, and pray for you till my dying day. *(Kneels to her and sobs.)* Ah!—a tear! it is alive! *(Runs to Triplet and hides her head.)* I am frightened! I am frightened!

Mrs. Warren's Profession

G.B. Shaw
1898

Scene: England

Dramatic
Mrs. Warren: a woman driven to prostitution by her need to survive, 40–50

When Mrs. Warren finally reveals the source of her income to her daughter, she explains why a young woman would turn to such a life.

MRS. WARREN: Everybody dislikes having to work and make money; but they have to do it all the same. I'm sure I've often pitied a poor girl, tired out and in low spirits, having to try to please some man that she doesn't care two straws for—some half-drunken fool that thinks he's making himself agreeable when he's teasing and worrying and disgusting a woman so that hardly any money could pay her for putting up with it. But she has to bear with disagreeables and take the rough with the smooth, just like a nurse in a hospital or anyone else. It's not work that any woman would do for pleasure, goodness knows; though to hear the pious people talk you would suppose it was a bed of roses. (…)
Of course it's worth while to a poor girl, if she can resist temptation and is good-looking and well conducted and sensible. It's far better than any other employment open to her. I always thought that oughtn't to be. It can't be right, Vivie, that there shouldn't be better opportunities for women. I stick to that: it's wrong. But it's so, right or wrong; and a girl must make the best of it. But of course it's not worth while for a lady. If you took to it you'd be a fool; but I should have been a fool if I'd taken to anything else.

The Philanderer

G.B. Shaw
1898

Scene: London

Dramatic
Julia: a young woman obsessed with a man of questionable morality, 20s

When the philandering Charteris announces that he wishes to end their relationship, Julia desperately begs him not to leave.

JULIA: But why? We could be so happy. You love me: I know you love me. I feel it. You say 'My dear' to me: you have said it several times this evening. I know I have been wicked, odious, bad: I say nothing in defense of myself. But don't be hard on me. I was distracted by the thought of losing you. I can't face life without you, Leonard. I was happy when I met you: I had never loved any one; and if you had only let me alone, I could have gone on contentedly by myself. But I can't now. I must have you with me. Don't cast me off without a thought of all I have at stake. I could be a friend to you if you would only let me; if you would only tell me your plans; give me a share in your work; treat me as something more than the amusement of an idle hour. Oh, Leonard, Leonard, you've never given me a chance: indeed you haven't. I'll take pains; I'll read; I'll try to think; I'll conquer my jealousy; I'll— *(She breaks down, rocking her head desperately on his knees and writhing.)* Oh, I'm mad: I'm mad: you'll kill me if you desert me.

Pillars of Society

Ibsen, Trans. by Rolf Fjelde

1877

Scene: a small Norwegian seaport

Dramatic

Martha Bernick: a woman who has just lost the man she loves to another, 70–80

All her life, Martha has loved Johan, who has just eloped with young Dina, a girl Martha has raised like her own daughter. Here, Martha finally reveals her feelings to Lona, Johan's sister.

MARTHA BERNICK: Yes, alone. So you might as well known—I've loved him more than anything on earth. (…)
The whole of my life is in those words. I loved him and waited for him. Every summer I waited for him to come. And then he came—but I didn't exist. (…)
What else could I do, when I loved him? Yes, I've loved him. My entire life has been lived for him, ever since he went away. You're thinking, what grounds did I have for hope? Oh, I believe I had some, all right. But when he came back—then it was as if everything had been wiped out of his memory. I didn't exist. (…)
[I'm glad she did.] When he left here, we were the same age. When I saw him again—oh, that horrible moment—I realized with a shock that now I was ten years older than he. Over there he'd been thriving in the bright, vibrant sunlight, drinking in youth and health with every breath; and meanwhile, here I'd been sitting indoors, spinning and spinning— (…)
Yes, it was gold I spun. No bitterness! Isn't it true, Lona, we've been like two good sisters to him.

Salome

Oscar Wilde
1894

Scene: the court of Herod

Dramatic
Salome: tempestuous daughter of Herodias, 16–20

Here, passionate young Salome escapes the stuffy confines of a royal banquet.

SALOME: How sweet is the air here! I can breathe here! Within there are Jews from Jerusalem who are tearing each other in pieces over their foolish ceremonies, and barbarians who drink and drink, and spill their wine on the pavement, and Greeks from Smyrna with painted eyes and painted cheeks, and frizzed hair curled in columns, and Egyptians silent and subtle, with long nails of jade and russet cloaks, and Romans brutal and coarse, with their uncouth jargon. Ah! how I loathe the Romans! They are rough and common, and they give themselves the airs of noble lords. (…)
How good to see the moon! She is like a little piece of money, a little silver flower. She is cold and chaste. I am sure she is a virgin. Yes, she is a virgin. She has never defiled herself. She has never abandoned herself to men, like the other goddesses.

Salome

Oscar Wilde
1894

Scene: the court of Herod

Dramatic
Salome: tempestuous daughter of Herodias, 16–20

After hearing the captive John the Baptist cry out, Salome becomes determined to see him. Here, she exerts her potent will on a guard.

SALOME: *(Going up to the young Syrian.)* Thou wilt do this thing for me, wilt thou not, Narraboth? Thou wilt do this thing for me. I have ever been kind towards thee. Thou wilt do it for me. I would but look at him, this strange prophet. Men have talked so much of him. Often I have heard the Tetrarch talk of him. I think he is afraid of him, the Tetrarch. Art thou, even thou, also afraid of him, Narraboth? (…)
Thou wilt do this thing for me, Narraboth, and to-morrow when I pass in my litter beneath the gateway of the idol-sellers I will let fall for thee a little flower, a little green flower. (…)
Thou wilt do this thing for me, Narraboth. Thou knowest that thou wilt do this thing for me. And on the morrow when I pass in my litter by the bridge of the idol-buyers, I will look at thee through the muslin veils, I will look at thee, Narraboth, it may be I will smile at thee. Look at me, Narraboth, look at me. Ah! thou knowest that thou wilt do what I ask of thee. Thou knowest it…I know that thou wilt do this thing.

Smiles and Tears; or,
The Widow's Stratagem

Marie-Therese DeCamp
1815

Scene: London

Dramatic
Cecil: a young woman forced to wander the streets of
London with her baby, 20s

*Lacking the protection of husband or family, Cecil must beg
in the streets of London in order to survive. Here, the destitute woman has reached the end of her endurance.*

CECIL: Your cries, at length, are hushed in sleep, my precious infant!
and cold and hunger are, for awhile, forgotten! How awful is
this silence! no sound falls on my ear, but the tumultuous beating of my frightened heart—lie still, lie still; your throbbings will
awake my babe—how comes this mist before my eyes? I'm very
faint—My child, my child! I can no longer bear your weight:
*(She sinks, placing the infant upon the trunk of one of the
trees.)* —What agony is this? numbed as my limbs are by the
stiffening blast, a scorching fire consumes my brain!—Can this
be fear? It is, the terror of a guilty conscience: there was a time,
when neither solitude nor night had power to terrify me—but I
was innocent then; then I had not offended Heaven, whose
protection I dare not now implore.—Ha! I hear a voice—Oh!
welcome, welcome sound!—Yet, should it be any one whom I
have known in other days—an idle fear; for if it should, night's
friendly shadows will conceal the features of the guilty Cecil—
I'll follow his footsteps—in common charity, he'll not deny that
comfort to a wretched, houseless wanderer!

The Ticket-Of-Leave Man

Tom Taylor

1863

Scene: London

Dramatic
May: a destitute young street singer, 20s

When a surly restaurant owner demands she leave his establishment, May calls him cruel, but then regrets her hasty remark.

MAY: *(Sinks down at one of the tables.)* I'm foolish to be angry, my bread depends on such as he. Oh, if I could only get away from this weary work! if some kind lady would take me in. I'm quick at my needle; but who'd take me, a vagabond, without a friend to speak for me? I'm all alone in the world now. It's strange how people's life is made for 'em. I see so many girls, nicely dressed, well off, with parents to love and care for 'em. I can't bear it sometimes, to see them, and then think what I am, and what's before me. *(Puts her hand to her face.)* I'm a silly girl: it's all because I'm so weak from the fever. There's nothing like keeping a good heart. How good he was to me; it was all through me he got into this trouble; but I mustn't think of him. Ah *(Looking off.)* there's a pleasant looking party younder. Come along old friend, you've to earn my supper yet.

The Ticket-Of-Leave Man

Tom Taylor
1863

Scene: London

Serio-Comic
Mrs. Willoughby: a pleasant busybody, 50–60

Here, a gregarious landlady entertains a tenant with a typical soliloquy.

MRS. WILLOUGHBY: I shall be much obliged to you, my dear—which I know when brothers and sisters meet they'll have a great deal to talk over and two's company and three's none, is well beknown—and I never was one to stand listenin' when other folks is talkin'—and one thing I may say, as I told Mrs. Molloy only last week, when the first floor had a little tiff with the second pair front about the water—'Mrs. Malloy,' I says, 'nobody ever heard me put in my oar when I wasn't asked,' I says, 'and idle chatterin', and gossip,' I says, 'is a thing that I never was given to, and I ain't a-goin to begin now,' I says, which good mornin' to you, young man, and a better girl, and a nicer girl, and a harder working girl than your sister, I 'ope and trust may never darken my doors. *(Brierly throws open door.)* Which her rent was ever ready to the day. No, my dear, it's the truth, and you needn't blush. *(During this last speech Brierly urges her towards the door.)* Thank you, *(Going to door.)* I can open the door for myself, young man. *(Turns to him.)* And a very nice looking head you have on your shoulders, though you have had your hair cut uncommon short, which I must say—good mornin', my dear, and anything I can do for you.

Uncle Tom's Cabin

George L. Aiken
1852

Scene: Simon Legree's Plantation in Louisiana

Dramatic
Cassy: Legree's slave and concubine, 20–30

*When Tom refuses to whip a fellow slave, Legree becomes
determined to break him. Here, Cassy begs Tom to give in
and save his life.*

CASSY: Don't call me missis. I'm a miserable slave like yourself—a
lower one than you can ever be! It's no use, my poor fellow,
this you've been trying to do. You were a brave fellow. You had
the right on your side; but it's all in vain for you to struggle. You
are in the Devil's hands; he is the strongest, and you must give
up. (…)
You see *you* don't know anything about it; I do. Here you are,
on a lone plantation, ten miles from any other, in the swamps;
not a white person here who could testify, if you were burned
alive. There's no law here that can do you, or any of us, the
least good; and this man! There's no earthly thing that he is not
bad enough to do. I could make one's hair rise, and their teeth
chatter, if I should only tell what I've seen and been knowing to
here; and it's no use resisting! Did I *want* to live with him?
Wasn't I a woman delicately bred? and he!—Father in Heaven!
what was he and is he? And yet I've lived with him these five
years, and cursed every moment of my life, night and day. (…)
And what are these miserable low dogs you work with, that
you should suffer on their account? Every one of them would
turn against you the first time they get a chance. They are all of
them as low and cruel to each other as they can be; there's no
use in your suffering to keep from hurting them?

The Bonds of Interest

Jacinto Benavente, Trans. by John Garrett Underhill
1907

Scene: a garden in an imaginary country

Serio-Comic
Dona Sirena: an outspoken aristocrat, 30s

*When informed that her servants will not work or entertain
at her pavilion until she pays them, Sirena rages.*

DONA SIRENA: Impudent rascal! Everything that I owe *him.* The
barefaced highwayman! And does he not stand indebted for his
reputation and his very credit in this city to me? Until I
employed him in the decoration of my person he did not know,
so to speak, what it was to dress a lady. (…)
The rogues! The brood of vipers! Whence does such insolence
spring? Were these people not born to serve? Are they to be
paid nowadays in nothing but money? Is money the only thing
which has value in the world? Woe unto her who is left without
a husband to look after her, as I am, without male relatives,
alas, without any masculine connection! A woman by herself is
worth nothing in the world, be she never so noble or virtuous.
O day foretold of the Apocalypse! Surely Antichrist has come!

Egon and Emilia

Christian Morgenstern
1901

Scene: a cozy living room

Serio-Comic
Emilia: an unfinished character, 20–30

When Egon refuses to speak to her, a dejected Emilia is forced to leave the stage, her passion unfulfilled.

EMILIA: *(Pulling Egon into the room by his hand.)* In here! That's right, in here, my darling Egon! Oh how happy I am, how happy your Emilia is! *(She gazes at Egon with eyes aglitter.)* But you say nothing at all— (…)
Have you no word for our happiness? But surely—*(She falters.)* (…) *(On the settle.)* I should have guessed it! I should have foreseen it! I'm a wretched creature! I'm a fool! But my God, all may not yet be lost—am I right, Egon *(She leaps up, in intense anguish.)* am I right, Egon? (…)
Oh, I implore you! Speak but a word, just one single little word! (…) *(At the round table.)* Oh, for heaven's sake—is it so impossible, this think I ask for, no beg for, plead for! I do not want your forgiveness or your understanding, no, not for a long while yet, we still have a good five acts for that, but let me have some point of contact, don't deny me some cue— (…)
(Out the window.) Egon! Egon!!—Egon!!! (…)
(To him.) Are you aware, shameless creature, that this is the death of me? That now I cannot develop into a character—all on account of your infamous silence? That I must now leave this stage, exit into the nameless void, without ever having acted or lived? *(She pulls out her watch and waits for a full minute.)* No answer, no inarticulate sound, not even a glance! Stone, stone, ice. Cruel wretch, you who have murdered my role, unnatural man, you who have strangled a domestic tragedy in its diapers…He is dumb, he sits there dumb, I go. Now, curtain, ring down once more, though you have scarcely been up; dear people, return home. You saw, I did what I could. All in vain. This brute wants no tragedy, he wants his peace and quiet. Farewell. *(Exits.)*

Enemies

Maxim Gorky, Trans. by Alexander Bakshy
1906

Scene: a garden

Dramatic
Tatyana: an actress, 28

As the world around her continues to change, Tatyana finds that she can no longer find the proper voice with which to inspire passion in an audience.

TATYANA: *(With disquiet.)* My province? I thought that as an actress I had solid ground under my feet—that I could reach the heights— *(Wearily yet forcefully.)* I feel uncomfortable, awkward in front of people who stare at me and say with cold eyes, "We know all that. It's old and boring." I feel weak, disarmed in front of them—I can't lay hold of them, arouse them. I want to tremble with fear or joy, I want to speak words charged with fire, passion, wrath—words that are sharp like knives, that burn like torches— I want to toss them lavishly, to strike awe in people! Let the people flare up, shout, rush out. But I can't find such words. Instead I toss them beautiful words, like flowers, words that are full of hope, happiness, love! They all cry—and I with them—we cry such fine tears. They applaud me, smother me with flowers, carry me in their arms. For a moment I reign over the people. In that moment is life—all life packed in one minute! But living words— I can't find.

The Florist Shop
Winifred Hawkridge
1915

Scene: Slovsky's Florist Shop

Serio-Comic
Maude: a talkative and philosophical shop girl, 20s

When Maude receives an order for flowers for a baby's funeral, she is prompted to ruminate on the florist shop's place in the lives of the community.

MAUDE: *(As the telephone rings.)* Hel-lo! This is Slovsky's. Yes'm, we make a specialty of tasteful offerings. *(Her voice drops to a tone of great sympathy.)* Soitenly, you kin leave it to us, and we will insure its being quiet and in good taste. If you'll just give me some idea of who the party was. *(Still greater sympathy.)* Oh! a little baby! Ain't that too bad. *(Sincerely.)* Well, we must look on these things as all for the best. I would suggest six dozen of them tiny white Mignon rosebuds, in a long spray, with white ribbon. The general effeck will be all green and white—light and pretty, and kinder innercent. *(Soothingly reassuring.)* Promptly at two—I'll see to it myself. *(Hangs up the receiver.)* Henry, ain't that sad? A little baby only six months old. I wonder what it died of? Teeth, prob'ly. (...)
(Earnestly.) In a way it ain't nothing, but I always get to thinking how it prob'ly suffered, and how the fam'ly suffered, and what it'd been like if it lived to grow up—and how what's jest "Two o'clock prompt" to Slovsky's is something like eternal doom to them, and what's jest 29 Main Street to Slovsky's errand boy is shelterin' thoity or forty souls in anguish. I like to think of them things, Henry. It makes the woik more interestin'. (...)
Up to the rubber fact'ry, now, I made two a week more, but I didn't git real life. But here—honest—I read to improve my mind, the way everyone ought to, but I often think Florence Barclay never wrote nothing half so sad or romantic as what goes on right under my nose.

The Hairy Ape
Eugene O'Neill
1922

Scene: a transatlantic ocean liner

Dramatic
Mildred: a passenger on an ocean liner, 20s

A member of the privileged class, Mildred has a desire to understand the life and needs of the common man as she here explains to her aunt.

MILDRED: *(Protesting with a trace of genuine earnestness.)* Please do not mock my attempts to discover how the other half lives. Give me credit for some sort of groping sincerity in that at least. I would like to help them. I would like to be some use in the world. Is it my fault I don't know how? I would like to be sincere, to touch life somewhere. *(With weary bitterness.)* But I'm afraid I have neither the vitality nor integrity. All that was burnt out in our stock before I was born. Grandfather's blast furnaces, flaming to the sky, melting steel, making millions—then father keeping those home fires burning, making more millions—and little me at the tail-end of it all! I'm a waste product in the Bessemer process—like the millions. Or rather, I inherit the acquired trait of the by-product, wealth, but none of the energy, none of the strength of the steel that made it. I am sired by gold and damned by it, as they say at the race track—damned in more ways than one. *(She laughs mirthlessly.)*

The Man Who Married a Dumb Wife

Anatole France
1915

Scene: Paris

Serio-Comic
Catherine: a woman who has just been "cured" of being
mute, 20

*Catherine's husband has taken great pains to see that she is
cured of her inability to speak. Unfortunately, his efforts
have backfired, for now the poor young woman can do
nothing but speak, as she here demonstrates.*

CATHERINE: My dear, we shall have for supper tonight some minced
mutton and what's left of that goose one of your suitors gave
us. Tell me, is that enough? Shall you be satisfied with it? I hate
being mean, and like to set a good table, but what's the use of
serving courses which will only be sent back to the pantry
untouched? The cost of living is getting higher all the time.
Chickens, and salads, and meats, and fruit have all gone up so,
it will soon be cheaper to order dinner sent in by a caterer. (…)
Yes, that's what we're coming to. No home life any more. You'll
see. Why, a capon, or a partridge, or a hare, cost less all stuffed
and roasted than if you buy them alive at the market. That is
because the cook-shops buy in large quantities and get a big
discount; so they can sell to us at a profit. I don't say we ought
to get our regular meals from the cook-shop. We can do our
everyday plain cooking at home, and it's better to; but when we
invite people in, or give a formal dinner party, then it saves time
and money to have the dinner sent in. Why, at less than an
hour's notice, the cook-shops and cake-shops will get you up a
dinner for a dozen, or twenty, or fifty people; the cook-shop
will send in meat and poultry, the caterer will send galantines
and sauces and relishes, the pastry-cook will send pies and tarts
and sweet desserts; and it's all so convenient. Now, don't you
think so yourself, Leonard?

A Man's World

Rachel Crothers
1909

Scene: New York City

Dramatic
Frank: an unconventional woman, 30s

*Frank has raised Kiddie as if he were her own son. Here,
she tells the sad tale of how Kiddie arrived in her home.*

FRANK: Kiddie has made me bitter. Poor little nameless fellow! I shall
never forget the night his mother came to us. I didn't know her
very well—she was only one of the hundreds of American girls
studying in Paris—but she came to me because she wanted to
get away from her own set. We kept her and she died when
Kiddie was born—and then we kept him—because we didn't
know what else in God's world to do with him—and then we
loved him—and after father died—somehow that poor, little,
helpless baby was the greatest comfort in the world to me. I
couldn't bear Paris without dad, so I came back to America.
Kiddie was two then, and we set up house in this old place
three years ago—and here we are—and it's nobody's business
who he is. I don't *know* who his father was; I don't *care* who
he was—but my name is better for the boy than his—for mine
is honest.

A Man's World

Rachel Crothers
1909

Scene: New York City

Dramatic
Clara: a struggling artist, 30s

*Clara has begun to despair of ever finding happiness in life.
When a friend asks why she never married, she makes the
following reply.*

CLARA: No man has ever asked me to marry him. I've never had a
beau—a real beau—in my life. I—I've always been superfluous
and plain. Absolutely superfluous. I'm not necessary to one single human being. I'm just one of those everlasting women that
the world is full of. There's nobody to take care of me and I'm
simply not capable of taking care of myself. I've tried—God
knows I've tried—and what is the use? What under Heaven do I
get out of it? If I were a man—the most insignificant little runt
of a man—I could persuade some woman to marry me—and
could have a home and children and hustle for my living—and
life would mean something. Oh, I can't bear it, Frank. I can't
bear it! I often wish I were pretty and bad and could have my
fling and die. *(Sobbing, she falls on the couch—huddled and
helpless.)*

Miss Lulu Bett

Zona Gale
1920

Scene: a middle class home

Dramatic
Lulu: a woman deceived cruelly by a man, 30s

When Lulu discovers that her new husband is already married, she plans to finally break free from his brother's family for whom she has just worked as a servant for years. Here, she finally tells the overbearing patriarch exactly what she thinks of the family and his lying brother.

LULU: Can't you understand anything? I've lived here all my life—on your money. I've not been strong enough to work they say—well, but I've been strong enough to be a hired girl in your house—and I've been glad to pay for my keep...But there wasn't a thing about it that I liked. Nothing about being here that I liked...Well, then I got a little something, same as other folks. I thought I was married and I went off on the train and he bought me things and I saw different towns. And then it was all a mistake. I didn't have any of it. I came back here and went into your kitchen again—I don't know why I came back. I suppose it's because I'm most thirty-four and new things ain't so easy any more—but what have I got or what'll I ever have? And now you want to put on to me having folks look at me and think he run off and left me and having them all wonder. I can't stand it. I can't stand it. I can't.... (...)
Yes. Because he wanted me. How do I know—maybe he wanted me only just because he was lonesome, the way I was. I don't care why. And I won't have folks think he went and left me.

On Vengeance Height

Allan Davis

1914

Scene: a primitive cabin in Tennessee

Dramatic
Gram: a blind mountain woman, 60s

*All of Gram's family with the exception of her grandson,
Clay, have been killed in a feud with a neighboring family.
When a well-meaning neighbor suggests that Clay will soon
have to take up arms himself, Gram reveals a family legacy
of blood and sorrow.*

GRAM: Go t' the winder an' look out—t' th' left. *(Hope does so.)*
That's Vengeance Height? (…)
Y' see somethin' 'ginst the sky? (…)
Some boulders 'bout's high's a man? (…)
Count 'em. (…) Count 'em. (…)
(Her sightless eyes gazing before her.) Thar's whar my man
Zeke's buried. 'Twar twenty year back. Er ol' sow of ourn had
done strayed away through a hole in the pen, an' the Carmalts
they claimed hit. The Carmalts—how I disgust that name! Zeke
went over t' see 'em 'bout it—friendly like. One thing led to
'nuther—thar war high words—an' old Jim Carmalt—he shot
Zeke—he shot him fr'm behin', without warnin' an' without a-
givin' him a chance....My Zeke—my man Zeke.... *(Living
through it again.)* I 'member w'en they fotched him thro' that
door, an' I turned down the kiver of that thar bed fer him, an'
they laid him on it, an' I tuk th' lint rags f'm this shelf an'
wropped him, and watched him an' watched. But the mornin'
o' th' next day, when it was a-gettin' gray thro' the winders, an'
the mockin' birds was a-whistlin' an' th' cuckoos a-callin', an'
the peckerwoods a-tappin, an' ev'rything was beginnin' agin
outside—he died. *(With grim but shaking interrogation.)* Thar's
anuther boulder beside that one, hain't thar? (…)
That's Jeff—my fust born. He killed Jim Carmalt as kilt his pap;
an' then Bryce Carmalt killed *him*. *(Pause. Then intensely.)* Go
on a-countin'— (…)

Them's my boys Steve and Tolliver. They war a-swimmin' one evenin' in Black Pool, an' Lem Carmalt, he shot 'em both, an' they died—in th' water— *(Hope turns away with a shudder.)* Why hain't yo' countin'? (…)

Yo' cain't count 'em, but I buried 'em, an' I kin count 'em…Th' nex' is five.…That war my boy Tom. He accounted fur *two* o' th' Carmalts afore they got him.…An' when he war a-dyin', I tol' him he done well, an' he went out a-smilin'. *(She pauses. Less strongly.)* An' the nex' is six…my boy Cliff—Clay's pappy. A mammy loves all her boys, but I reckon I loved Cliff mos'—he hed curly chestnut hair an' war allers bright an' smilin' an'—oh, he war jes'—*Cliff*…He war a-takin' me ter th' Gap. Hit war 'bout this time o' year. The milkweed pods war a-bustin' an' thar war asters an' gentian, an' barberry bresh red's a flannel shirt in th' woods an' th' golden ragwort war a-shinin' clean an' yeller. How good I cud see in them days—how good I cud see!…I wuz on hoss-back behin' Cliff, an' he war a-singin'. Then sudden a turkey-buzzar' riz up a-tween the hoss's hoffs— an' afore I cud even think how bad a sign it wuz, Lem Carmalt an' two more of 'em done fired at us.…Cliff got one of them— an' then—they shot Cliff—an' w'en I see him layin' theer so still, I tuk his Win-chester an' shot Bryce Carmalt— *(Pause. Slowly.)* An' then Lem Carmalt he fired at me—an'—I lost my eyes. *(Simply—as if summing it all up.)* An' thar war six boulders on Vengeance Height in our plot, an' five in th' Carmalts' plot— an' me. *(With a change.)* That's why w'en th' circuit rider asked me t' give him Clay t' take to school w'en he war ten year old, I let him go. That's why I've kep' him away these six years—t' keep him safe.… *(With an outcry of stifled grief and loneliness.)* D' yo' reckon I relish my little gran'son t' be away? D' yo' reckon I relish t' live hyar all alone, blin' an' helpless? But I'm gettin' old. I cain't stand things ez I could…Clay's all I got, and I'm scairt fur him—scairt o' that rattlesnake Lem Carmalt as killed my boys Steve an' Tolliver an' Cliff an' tuk away my sight—I'm scairt…I'm scairt.…

Servitude

Eugene O'Neill
1914

Scene: a home in Tarryville-on-Hudson, NY

Dramatic
Alice Roylston: a woman convinced her husband is having an affair, 30–40

Here, unhappy Alice confronts the woman she has convinced herself is having an affair with her husband.

ALICE: I won't break down again. What must be, must be, I suppose. I have known this was coming for a long time. The day I was married I could foresee it. I should have had the courage to refuse then; but I didn't. It all seemed such a wonderful dream come true, I just couldn't refuse even when I knew I was wronging him. I was a coward then and I still am, I guess. Eleven years of happiness and now I have to pay and—I am afraid. *(A pause, during which Mrs. Frazer looks at her pityingly.)* I've pretended not to see a lot of things in those years. I wanted him to be happy, and I knew he wouldn't be if he thought he had a jealous wife prying into his affairs. All the women who sent him flowers and wrote to him and called him up on the phone—I knew they loved him, and I hated them for it; but I never let him think I suspected anything. Until lately I never thought he considered them seriously. (…)
He used to read parts of their letters to me. He never guessed how it hurt. For I could see in spite of the way he joked they pleased him just the same. Then all at once he stopped showing them to me—and they kept coming, all in the same handwriting. I had never read a letter of his before but I brooded until I couldn't resist the temptation any longer. Two of them were lying open on this table one day and I read them. Then I could see the end coming. He had been writing to her, meeting her in New York, and I knew from the letters it was only a question of time.

Torches

Kenneth Raisbeck
1920

Scene: Italy, 15th century

Serio-Comic
Gismonda: a flirtatious young wife, 18

Gismonda regrets having married an older man and leaving Rome as she here indicates.

GISMONDA: *(Angrily crying.)* Oh, why did I ever leave Rome? In Rome were plays, tourneys, masques, dancing. In Rome I was loved! In Rome there were men to whom my favor was of more moment than a cameo or a parchment! I am freezing here! Say my lord loves me—Is it as a woman should be loved? Is it I who count always first with him, more to him than his whole world? Oh, I know that I have value! I count among his treasures! I adorn his museum along with other such treasures as this fan, that statue, or that, or that, or this tinted Murano glass! *(She holds up the wine glass.)* Yes, doubtless my rank is equal with this goblet! Or less exalted, for he got me gratis in Rome, with a dowry beside, while he got this crystal from Murano and paid a great price for it!

Torches

Kenneth Raisbeck
1920

Scene: Italy, 15th century

Dramatic
Gismonda: a flirtatious young wife, 18

*When her husband discovers her affair with the young
Pietro, he commands that she drink a cup of poison after
first placing a ruby that she has long desired in the cup.
After drinking the poison and gaining the ruby, Gismonda
bids farewell to the world.*

GISMONDA: Rome would envy me this ruby! Bury it with me; I would
have it burn among my dust— *(A short pause; in a low voice;
smiling.)* When I am dust! *(She sways. The wine glass falls from
her hand and breaks.)* Pardon, Signor connoisseur! It was a
thing you loved—Murano glass, beautiful, like me, and easily
broken. We shall put lip to lip again, that cup and I, in— *(She
laughs.)* Dante's Hell? *(She sits in the chair by the table.)* To die
of my first affair! That's droll enough! In Rome they will say you
might as well have killed me for wearing my hat in the fashion!
In Rome we are less finicking! I was a Roman.... *(With a kind of
pleased surprise.)* That's my epitaph! *(Silence; then fretfully.)* I
am cold! *(Alessandro silently brings the silks and velvets, and
lays them about her shoulders, and over her knees and feet.)*
That foolish song keeps running in my head— *(Singing feebly.)*
    "Love us enough!
    Plead not! More is not mine to give—"
That makes me think of one who was ready to die of love for
me—

The Web

Eugene O'Neill
1913–14

Scene: a squalid bedroom of a rooming house on the lower east side of Manhattan

Dramatic
Rose: an ailing prostitute, 22

With a baby, no money, an abusive man, and failing health, Rose's prospects don't look very good. When a kindly stranger asks why she doesn't give up a prostitutes life, she makes the following reply.

ROSE: *(Wearily.)* Talk is cheap. Yuh don't know what you're talkin' about. What job c'n I git? What am I fit fur? Housework is the only thing I know about and I don't know much about that. Where else could I make enough to live on? That's the trouble with all us girls. Most all of us ud like to come back but we jest can't and that's all there's to it. We can't work out of this life because we don't know how to work. We was never taught how. *(She shakes with a horrible fit of coughing, wipes her lips, and smiles pitifully.)* Who d'yuh think would take chance on hiring me the way I look and with this cough? Besides, there's the kid. *(Sarcastically.)* Yuh may not know it but people ain't strong for hirin' girls with babies—especially when the girls ain't married.

The Women

Clare Boothe
1936

Scene: New York City

Serio-Comic
Sylvia: a society busybody, 30s

When nosy Sylvia pays a visit to a friend who happens to be taking a shower, her need to snoop far outweighs her sense of propriety.

SYLVIA: *(Sees the scales, decides to weigh herself.)* Oh, dear, I've lost another pound. I must remember to tell my analyst. You know, everything means something. *(The shower goes on. Helene exits. Sylvia gets off the scales. During the following monologue, she goes to Crystal's dressing-table, where she examines all the bottles and jars.)* But even my analyst says no woman should try to do as much as I do. He says I attach too much value to my feminine friendships. He says I have a Damon and Pythias Complex. I guess I have given too much of myself to other women. He says women are natural enemies— *(Picks up bottle.)* Why, Crystal, I thought you didn't touch up your hair— *(Sniffing perfume.)* My dear, I wouldn't use this. You smell it on every tart in New York. That reminds me— *(Going to the shower-curtain.)* —if you do have an affair, Crystal, for heaven's sake, be discreet. Remember what Howard did to me, the skunk. *(Peeking in.)* My, you're putting on weight. *(Going back to dressing-table, she sits down, and begins to pry in all the drawers.)* But mean are so mercenary. They think they own you body and soul, just because they pay the bills—I tried this cream. It brought out pimples—Of course, Crystal, if you were smart, you'd have a baby. It's the only real hold a woman has—

Business Lunch at the Russian Tea Room

Christopher Durang
1994

Scene: the Russian Tea Room

Serio-Comic
Melissa: a Hollywood development person, 30s

Here, Hollywood and New York combine with predictable results as Melissa does her best to court a playwright for movie work.

MELISSA: Christopher, all of us at Zerofax feel that we want to return to the old-fashioned kind of movie where the characters have dialogue and thoughts and emotions—you know like *Four Weddings and a Funeral,* we think that was great, you know, Hugh Grant and romance and people buying tickets. That's what it's about, and that's what makes Zerofax a different kind of movie company. We're interested in quality. (…)
Oh, that's right. Well, he wasn't available, so then we called you. My assistant Jane loves your work, she said, why don't you call Christopher, he's a very funny writer. And I thought that was a brilliant idea. (…)
I love theatre writers. I produced "Sleaze-O-Rama" for television last year. Did you see it? It got great numbers. It was about a serial killer who became president but who found his humanity after he got AIDS and died. Everyone loved it. Lanford Wilson wrote the first script, which was beautiful, but we had to throw it out because none of the network people liked it, so we had Babaloo Feldman rewrite every single word. But Lanford understood. He thought we wanted something sensitive, but we didn't. I hope he brings the caviar soon, I have a meeting with Nora Ephron in 15 minutes. Nora Ephron is the kind of quality writer we want to work with. That's why I'm meeting with you as well. (…)
We want Nora to write a move for Meg Ryan where Meg is a widow who misses her husband dreadfully, they had this really

special relationship, and then some man hears her talking on the radio, and he's really moved by what she says and he wants to contact her, but the switch is it's her husband who hears her on the radio, she's not a widow at all, he disappeared at sea just like Julia Roberts did in the movie watcha-ma-call-it, and then he shows up and he kills her. It's sort of like *Sleepless in Seattle* meets "Psycho." What was that Julia Roberts' movie called?

The Danube

Maria Irene Fornes
1986

Scene: in the garden

Dramatic
Eve: a woman trying to say good-bye to the man she loves,
20–30

*Eve here begs Paul to leave even though she knows she
can't let go.*

Eve: This may be the last time I come here.
    Here is where I first kissed you.
    I kissed you that day, you know.
    I kissed you because I could not help myself.
    Now again I try to exert control over myself
    and I can't.
    I try to appear content and I can't.
    I know I look distressed.
    I feel how my face quivers. And my blood feels thin.
    And I can hardly breathe. And my skin feels dry.
    I have no power to show something other than what I feel.
    I am destroyed. And even if I try,
    my lips will not smile.
    Instead I cling to you and make it harder for you.
    Leave now.
    Leave me here looking at the leaves.
    Good-bye.
    If I don't look at you it may be that I can let you go.

Desire, Desire, Desire

Christopher Durang

1987

Scene: a shabby New Orleans apartment

Serio-Comic
Cora: a good time gal, 30–50

*Here, Cora regales Stanley and Blanche with a tale about
pipe dreams in a parody of the work of Tennessee Williams.*

CORA: Hiya, everybody. Bejees, me and Pearl was just at Harry Hope's
saloon talkin' about pipe dreams, and Hickey came in for his
usual bender, and he told his iceman story that he tells every
year, and then he said we all had too many pipe dreams, and
when Chuck and me talked about our pipe dream of savin' up
enough money to get married and live on a farm if only Chuck
could stay on the wagon for a coupla weeks, Hickey looked at
us with this kinda mean smile on his ugly map, and he said,
beejees, *pipe dreams,* you kids run your life wid *pipe dreams,*
but I just killed my wife and now I don't got no *pipe dreams,*
and, Pearl, you'd be better off without *pipe dreams* too, and so
Chuck and me realize, we did have a *pipe dream* our lives
would get better, but now we see that ain't gonna happen, I'm
a whore and he's a drunk. But at least we ain't got no pipe
dreams anymore!

The End of the Day

Jon Robin Baitz
1992

Scene: Los Angeles

Dramatic
Rosamund Brackett: Director of an impoverished medical
clinic, 60s

*When Brackett fires one of her doctors (an expatriate Brit
with a bad attitude), she is shocked to discover that he has
an original painting by Stubbs in his office. Here, she
explains her love for the artist.*

ROSAMUND BRACKETT: Is that a Stubbs? *(She looks at the painting carefully.)* This is a real George Stubbs? (…)
It's so great. (…)
It breaks my heart in two that a despicable little fop like you
should possess such a thing. A waste. (…)
Oh I've always had a flame for Stubbs. I went to London twen-
ty-four years ago and I saw "A Comparative Anatomical
Exposition of the Structure of the Human Body with that of a
Tiger and a Common Fowl." We're so different. And he made
that clear, but the same too. The same. And—and exquisite—
all. Even his realization, in the painting of a horse—say—of the
preoccupations of a dying class. There we all are. In the painting. *(She smiles.)* My husband. He took me. He started this
place. But he died. He'd have hated you. Taken you out into the
courtyard and thrashed you to within an inch of your life then
prayed over your broken body and wept. That was him. You'd
have adored him. *(Bracket pours herself a drink and lights a
smoke. She looks out the window at San Pedro's twinkling
lights.)* That painting has the scent of my husband. Too bad.
Decent man. Decent man. What a time. None left. I wasn't
much of anything before I met my husband and I'm pretty
thinned out without him, but he was decent. *(She turns to
Massey, imploring.)* Why is that so impossible to ask for in anyone now? Why is that, doctor? Why is it that nothing…works?

We all know it—you're quite right, you know. I feel so proud of myself for sticking it out down here. Every time one of them dies, Graydon...I feel stronger. Isn't that horrible? Every time one of them dies, I feel like one of those women on the prairie, moving out west, being brave. Ugly. So ugly... *(Beat.)* Is wanting to help people so silly?

Gemini

Alberto Innaurato
1978

Scene: a neighborhood in Philadelphia, 1973

Serio-Comic
Bunny: a loud and vulgar woman, 40s

Bunny here describes the terrible events that led to her being charged with assault.

BUNNY: I'm eatin' light, got stage fright. Gotta go a court today. (…) That bitch, Mary O'Donnel, attacked me. I was lyin' there, mindin' my own business, and she walks in, drops the groceries, screams, then throws herself on top of me. (…) [Whataya mean: Who's bed?] Don't matter who's bed. No matter where a person is, that person gotta right to be treated wit courtesy. And her fuckin' husband was no use; he just says: Oh, Mary! turns over and goes back to sleep. So's I hadda fend for myself. She threw herself on top of me, see, so I broke her fuckin' arm. Well, you woulda thought the whole world was fuckin' endin'. She sat there and screamed. I didn't know what to do. It was her house. I didn't know where nothin' was and she's a shitty housekeeper. So I shook her fuckin' husband's arm and said get the fuck up I just broke your fuckin' wife's arm. But he shook me off, you know how these men are, afta, so's I put on my slip, and I put on my dress and got the hell out of there. I'll tell you my ears was burnin'. That witch has gotta tongue like the murders in the Rue Morgue. Then, all of a face, she's got the guts to go to the cops and say I assaulted her. Well, I was real ashamed to have to admit I did go after Mary O'Donnel. She smells like old peanuts. Ever smell her, Lucille? (…)
So's I gotta go to court and stand trial. But I ain't worried. I gotta uncle on the force, he's a captain. Come on, Herschel. Sam the Jew wan's a see his kid today.

Imperceptible Mutabilities

Suzan-Lori Parks

1989

Scene: here and now

Dramatic
Verona: a fan of Mutual of Omaha's Wild Life Kingdom, 30s

Here, Verona shares a disturbing memory.

VERONA: I saw my first pictures of Africa on TV: Mutual of Omaha's *Wild Kingdom*. The thirty-minute filler between Walt Disney's wonderful world and the CBS *Evening News*. It was a wonderful world: Marlin Perkins and Jim and their African guides. I was a junior guide and had a lifesize poster of Dr. Perkins sitting on a white Land Rover surrounded by wild things. Had me an 8 x 10 glossy of him too, signed, on my nightstand. Got my nightstand from Sears cause I had to have Marlin by my bed at night. Together we learned to differentiate African from Indian elephants the importance of hyenas in the wild funny looking trees on the slant—how do they stand up? Black folks with no clothes. Marlin loved and respected all the wild things. His guides took his English and turned it into the local lingo so that he could converse with the natives. Marlin even petted a rhino once. He tagged the animals and put them into zoos for their own protection. He encouraged us to be kind to animals through his shining example. Once there was uh me name Verona: I got mommy n dad tuh get me uh black dog n named it I named it "Namib" after thuh African sands n swore tuh be nice tuh it only Namib refused tuh be trained n crapped in corners of our basement n got up on thuh sofa when we went out n Namib wouldn't listen tuh me like Marlins helpers listened tuh him Namib wouldn't look at me when I talked tuh him n when I said someuhn like "sit" he wouldn't n "come" made im go n when I tied him up in thuh front yard so that he could bite the postman when thuh postman came like uh good dog would he wouldn't even bark just smile n wag his tail so I would kick Namib when no one could see me cause I was sure I was very

very sure Namib told lies uhbout me behind my back and Namib chewed through his rope one day n bit me n run off. I have this job. I work at a veterinarian hospital. I'm a euthanasia specialist! Someone brought a stray dog in one day and I entered "black dog" in the black book and let her scream and whine and wag her tail and talk about me behind my back then I offered her the humane alternative. Wiped her out! I stayed late that night so that I could cut her open because I had to see I just had to see the heart of such a disagreeable domesticated thing. But no. Nothing different. Everything in place. Do you know what that means? Everything in its place. That's all.

Keely and Du

Jane Martin
1993

Scene: a basement

Dramatic
Keely: a pregnant woman, 20–30

Keely has been kidnapped by a group of radical anti-abor-
tion protesters who intend to keep her prisoner until she is
forced to give birth to the baby she doesn't want. Here, the
furious Keely expresses her feeling to her jailer.

KEELY: *(Flaring.)* Hey, I didn't choose to have this baby. (…)
[And I'm here.] I don't have, you know, Bible reading to hold up. I'm
not some lawyer, all right, with this argument, that argument,
put in this clause, fix the world. I can't do this, take care of my
dad, get myself straight, take on a baby, I got, you know, night-
mares, stuff like that, I see, whatsername, Princess Di, on some
supermarket magazine, I'm there crying, they have to call the
manager, because what we've got here, I could get messed up,
who knows, killed by who impregnated me, not to mention I
might, I don't know, hate this baby, hurt this baby, throw the
baby or something like that, I'm not kidding, what's inside me.
Now, do you have some Bible quotes for that, or am I just
beside the point, handcuffed to this bed, carrying the results of
being fucked by my ex-husband while he banged my head off a
hardwood floor to shut me up.

Look Back In Anger

John Osborne
1956

Scene: a one-room flat in the Midlands

Dramatic
Alison: a young woman who has just lost a baby, 20s

Alison left her emotionally abusive husband, Jimmy, when she discovered she was pregnant. Months later, she has lost the baby and returns to Jimmy, who still views her departure as a betrayal. Here, Alison finally breaks down in front of Jimmy and reveals her darkest self.

ALISON: It doesn't matter! I was wrong, I was wrong! I don't want to be neutral, I don't want to be a saint. I want to be a lost cause. I want to be corrupt and futile! *(Her voice takes on a little strength, and rises.)* Don't you understand? It's gone! It's gone! That—that helpless human being inside my body. I thought it was so safe, and secure in there. Nothing could take it from me. It was mine, my responsibility. But it's lost. *(She slides down against the leg of the table to the floor.)* All I wanted was to die. I never knew what it was like. I didn't know it could be like that! I was in pain, and all I could think of was you, and what I'd lost. *(Scarcely able to speak.)* I thought: if only—if only he could see me now, so stupid, and ugly and ridiculous. This is what he's been longing for me to feel. This is what he wants to splash about in! I'm in the fire, and I'm burning, and all I want is to die! It's cost him his child, and any others I might have had! But what does it matter—this is what he wanted from me! *(She raises her face to him.)* Don't you see! I'm in the mud at last! I'm groveling! I'm crawling! Oh, God—

The Marriage of Bette and Boo

Christopher Durang
1985

Scene: here and now

Dramatic
Bette: a woman obsessed with having children, 40–50

Here, Matt fantasizes what his mother would say about her unrelenting quest to have children.

BETTE: You're the only one of my children that lived. You should see me more often. (…)
You're right. It's not fair of me to bring up the children that died; that's beside the point. I realize Boo and I must take responsibility for our own actions. Of course, the Church wasn't very helpful at the time, but nonetheless we had brains of our own, so there's no point in assigning blame. I must take responsibility for wanting children so badly that I foolishly kept trying over and over, hoping for miracles. Did you see the article in the paper, by the way, about how they've discovered a serum for people with the Rh problem that would have allowed me to have more babies if it had existed back then? (…)
[Yes I did.] It made me feel terribly sad for a little while; but then I thought, what's past is past. One has no choice but to accept facts. And I realized that you must live your own life, and I must live mine. My life may not have worked out as I wished, but still I feel a deep and inner serenity, and so you mustn't feel bad about me because I am totally happy and self sufficient in my pretty sunlit apartment. And now I'm going to close my eyes, and I want you to go out into the world and live your life. Good-bye. God bless you. *(Closes her eyes.)*

Moonlight
Harold Pinter
1993

Scene: here and now

Dramatic
Bridget: a restless spirit, 30s

*Here, Bridget wanders quietly through her parent's house
on the night her father is die.*

BRIDGET: Once someone said to me—I think it was my mother or my
father—anyway, they said to me—We've been invited to a
party. You've been invited too. But you'll have to come by yourself, alone. You won't have to dress up. You just have to wait
until the moon is down. *(Pause.)* They told me where the party
was. It was in a house at the end of a lane. But they told me
the party wouldn't begin until the moon had gone down.
(Pause.) I got dressed in something old and I waited for the
moon to go down. I waited a long time. Then I set out for the
house. The moon was bright and quite still. *(Pause.)* When I got
to the house it was bathed in moonlight. The house, the glade,
the lane, were all bathed in moonlight. But the inside of the
house was dark and all the windows were dark. There was no
sound. *(Pause.)* I stood there in the moonlight and waited for
the moon to go down.

Park Your Car in Harvard Yard

Israel Horovitz
1992

Scene: East Gloucester, Massachusetts

Dramatic
Kathleen: an Irish Catholic Yankee, Gloucester native, 40s

*Kathleen now works for Jacob Brackish, a man she has
secretly hated for having an affair with her mother. Now in
his 80s and nearly deaf, Jacob is no longer the formidable
school teacher he once was. Here, Kathleen vents some
spleen, knowing full well that Brackish can't hear her.*

KATHLEEN: I'm bringin' your tea up! *(No reply.)* Hullo? *(She climbs the
stairs to Brackish's room, pauses at the door, seemingly unno-
ticed by Brackish, who continues reading, his back to Kathleen.
She tests his deafness.)* Hullo? Your hearin'-aid in or out or
what? Hullo? *(No reply.)* Hullooooo! *(Kathleen enters Brackish's
room. She slams door closed to test his hearing. He doesn't
respond at all. She pauses, directly behind him, out of his line of
vision. She stares at him, silently, five count. Satisfied that he
cannot hear her, Kathleen speaks into his deafness.)* Sometimes,
I am just amazed to think that I'm standing here and you're just
there, within striking distance and all. You're like a legend to
me, really…If my father could see me now. Wouldn't he'd
a'b'en the jealous one, huh? I mean, he use'ta' dream a 'bein'
this close ta' you…and havin' a rock in his hand, a'course!…He
was interested in marine biology, my father. He loved the sea
and the boats and all. He always loved ta' point out different
kinds'a weeds and name the fish and all…especially down the
marshes. You'd think you were listenin' to some kind'a Hav'id
professor, or somesuch. It really pisses me off ta' think that he
spent his life, workin' the docks, lumpin', as he did. It killed him
young, carryin' crates in Win'tah, and all. Deadhead stupid
labor. Stupid, stupid useless!…He use'ta get tanked up, wick'id,
down ta' Sherm's…he'd come home and beat my mother…I
know he would'a loved to have beaten you, Brackish, but, the
closest he could ever come was ta' beat my mother. The three

of us girls cowerin' in the corner…like mice, scared shit so wick-'id bad…Nobody havin' a life worth livin'…Every time I heard your name out loud, Brackish, it was in connection with somebody like my father gettin' their hearts broken, gettin' flunked, gettin' creamed. Nobody was ever good enough…smart enough…worth sendin' on inta' the world…You musta' hated passin' the ones you had'ta' pass: the John Connors and the Annie Bells…the naturally-smart-student-types. Most'a us scared little bastids, us poor lumpers' kids, we didn't stand a chance, did we? Not a chance!

Songs of Love

Romulus Linney
1986

Scene: the Woodvale Nursing Home, Madison, Tennessee,
1986

Serio-Comic
Lillian Barbow: A southern matron, 50s

*When Lillian discovers that her mother is having a sexual
relationship with a fellow patient at the nursing home, she
and her brother rush in to put a stop to things. When the
aged lovers inform their children that they intend to leave
the nursing home and get married, Lillian does her best to
dissuade her mother from what she feels is an unacceptable
course of action.*

LILLIAN: Mother, marriage is a serious step. *(Susan laughs. Finley
laughs.)* Please! (…)
Mother, you can't have know Mr. Runney— (…)
Lieutenant Colonel Runney—for very long. You haven't been
here six months yourself. You could make a dreadful mistake. (…)
Mother, it's very hard when you won't talk to me. I am your
daughter, Lillian, who's done more for you than—and never
mind that, just stop with these silly cards and speak to me! (…)
It isn't just getting married. It's doing it without telling us, or
consulting us. If we hadn't come here today, what would you
have done? Just driven off with him? (…)
You understand, Mother, marriage, even at your age, means
sex? You would have to submit to this man's carnal desires? (…)
Mother, this is your daughter speaking. I know you better than
this. You are not a promiscuous woman. You had your children
and you moved into your own bedroom and slept by yourself in
peace and dignity, and I admired you for it. I have done exactly
the same. It is a great relief. But now you will have to
accommodate a man again. This man, with real or imaginary sexual
needs. (…)
You put that down!! *(She smiles, and speaks calmly.)* Mother,
this is the point. You have been put in this home by your loving

children because the plain fact is, you can't take care of yourself any more. Remember the lost check books? Yes. Remember the missed appointments you couldn't remember you made? Yes. Remember the forgotten house, which you lived in for sixty years and one pretty day couldn't find? Yes. Remember the telephone calls to people dead thirty years and front doors left open and the burned food, the gas from the oven blowing up in your face, and the kitchen, pantry and dining room in flames? Yes. And now you want to get married, to upset the practical arrangements so carefully made for you. You are thinking about no one but yourself. What will you do? Take half your estate from your children and grandchildren, and give it to a man you hardly know? Next you'll want to make a new will, and give it all away! No. You are incompetent, Mother, and you are staying here.

The Substance of Fire
Jon Robin Baitz
1990

Scene: New York City, the present

Dramatic
Marge Hackett: a woman starting a new life, 50s

*Marge's late husband was involved in a city government
scandal which left her a penniless widow. Now, Marge
works for social services. She has been sent to evaluate
Isaac Geldhart, a man whom she once met socially when
they were both living happier lives. His children would like
to have him committed to an old age home. She expected
to find a senile, incompetent old man but discovers instead
a bitter old man who is being victimized by his children.*

MARGE: I'm not waiting for anything. In the last five years I put
myself through school and got this job, which, admittedly is not
what I imagined, but still. What have you *done,* lately? I had to
drive out to Long Island with a suit for my husband, because he
was wearing jogging pants and a Drexel Burnham T-shirt when
they found him. *(Pause.)* What chance do I have? Fuck you.
Man, I hope I don't look fragile or give the impression that I'm
on some sort of widow's walk. I have a son who knows his
father ripped off everything in this city that wasn't nailed down!
I watched my husband on news at five, *weeping.* Chance?
What chance do I have? Because I won't have dinner with you?
(Beat.) Do you know how much I hate having dinner by myself
night after night? Well, I'd rather do that, let me assure you,
than have dinner with you and compare bad-break notes. (…)
We are nothing alike. Whatever has happened to you, you've
done to yourself. You had everything and you threw it away.

Summer

Jane Martin
1984

Scene: Montana, 1949

Serio-Comic
Dilly: a pistol, bright and cosseted, 18

Dilly's father breeds roosters for cockfights. Here she describes the handler's experience.

DILLY: He says he likes best to see the chickens die. (…)
He says this… *(The scars.)* is what handling is. The gaffs are up to three inches long and sharp as a razor…sharper. The cocks get crazy when they see each other. They twist in your arms and cut you. You bring them up, let 'em peck, get 'em nuts. Take 'em back six feet. It's a dirt floor. Floodlights. Cut-judge signals you turn 'em loose. They fly and hit. Slash each other. Lot of times the gaffs get caught in their flesh. Then you catch 'em. Say your gaffs are in my rooster. Then it's my job to take them out. Slowly. Gently. No mistakes. Here is where a gaff goes through his hand when he does this. The other handler, his cousin, pulled it out. One time this guy thinks he dopes the chickens so later when he watches another fight, the guy trips him into the pit and he falls on the chickens and they cut him and cut him and cut him. His uncle has a pickle factory so his father takes him there and makes him lie with the pickles in the brine to stop the blood and seal the wound. *(Dilly laughs.)* He wouldn't eat pickles if he were you.

The Taking of Miss Janie
Ed Bullins
1974

Scene: California, the 60s

Dramatic
Janie: a college student, 20s

Janie and Monty have been friends for a while. When Monty, who is black, responds to Janie's interest sexually, she accuses him of raping her.

JANIE: *(Not looking at him at first.)* It's sad...so sad...I don't even understand it...Once you said...no...no...many times you've told me...that anything's possible...But I wouldn't believe you. I *couldn't* believe you...You made the world, life, people...*everything*...seem so grim...And I knew it couldn't be that way...It couldn't...Even while I felt sad most of the time. Even while I suffered and had what you called "The Blues."...Even though I didn't understand why you refused to give into sadness...to feeling down and beat...I...I still didn't believe, Monty. I didn't. I still didn't believe that I have so little understanding of the world....Oh, Monty, I have so little understanding of people and life...and I don't know *you*, who I thought was my friend, at all...And now...and now I don't know what's going to happen to me...We've been friends for such a long time. Such a long time...Ten years...? God, it's been that long....I don't know what I'll do now....I don't know what's going to happen to me....For such a long time I thought of you as one of my few friends. A special friend, really. Do you understand that, Monty?...My special friend...And now you rape me...you rape me! *(She begins to cry softly. Monty raises his head from the pillow, then reaches over and pulls her to him and kisses her until she quiets. She doesn't resist. Janie catches her breath.)* Oh, Monty...Monty...why...why?

The Taking of Miss Janie

Ed Bullins
1974

Scene: California, the 60s

Dramatic
Janie: a college student, 20s

*Here, repressed Janie does her best to justify her attraction
to Monty.*

JANIE: *(Smokes a joint, ladylike.)* I'm not really lonely. At least so I
would know it. But there's not many people I can relate to...or
even talk to. That's why I like Monty as a friend. He's nice.
Sensitive. Serious. And with so much talent. That's why I can't
allow him to get too close to me. I want him as a friend. That's
all. It's not because of Lonnie. I'm tired of Lonnie. But he's like a
bad habit I can't shake. I once thought he was the one for me.
But I was younger and more innocent and didn't realize the vast
differences and problems that lay between us. Lonnie will never
be anything more than Lonnie, I guess, he'll never have a big
name in jazz. Never really do more than be a second-rate side-
man at the Whiskey A-Go-Go. So it isn't Lonnie that keeps me
from letting Monty has his way with me. Nor is it because
Monty's black and I'm white. Gee...I think colored people are
neat. And I've made it with black guys before. And I guess I'll
do it some more. But not with Monty. He's a friend. A lifelong
friend, I hope. And I know that men and women more often
than not sacrifice their friendships when they become lovers. So
I'll be true to Monty. To keep our friendship alive. And perhaps
our relationship with mature into the purest of loves one day.
An ideal black/white love. Like sweet grapes change with age
and care into a distinctive bouquet upon choice, rare wines.

The Value of Names

Jeffrey Sweet
1982

Scene: Malibu, the early 1980s

Serio-Comic
Norma: an actress, 30s

*Here, the daughter of a well-known character actor
describes how she discovered that he had been black-listed
in Hollywood.*

NORMA: *(To audience.)* I was fifteen years old, pushing a shopping
cart at the A&P, when I found out what he'd been through.
There were two people standing on line ahead of me, so I
checked out the magazine rack to see what I could waste a few
minutes with. And there was a caricature of my father grinning
out at me from the cover of *TV Guide.* At the bottom it said,
"Benny Silverman of *Rich But Happy.*" That was the name of
the situation comedy he played a crazy neighbor on—*Rich But
Happy.* So, of course I'm eager to see what it has to say about
him. Maybe he'll mention me or Mom, though at that point
they'd been divorced already ten years or so. So I'm standing on
line at the A&P, smiling, reading about how he's buddies with all
the technicians on the set, about a practical joke he played on
the producer once, about how the younger actors on the show
revere him as a comic genius, and so forth and so on. And then
there was this classic *TV Guide* transitional sentence. Something
about—"But Benny Silverman still has vivid memories of the
black days when his chief concern was not fine-tuning a laugh
but fighting for the right to practice his craft." This was followed by how he was named in front of the House Committee
on Un-American Activities. And how he had been subpoenaed
to appear, and how he did appear but did not cooperate. And
then, years of not being able to find work. I was in the middle
of this when it was my turn at the checkout counter. I paid for
the groceries, and I took them home and dumped them on the
kitchen table. And I asked my mother whether it had been by
planning or oversight that nobody had ever told me a word
about it.

Victory on Mrs. Dandywine's Island

Lanford Wilson
1970

Scene: an island

Serio-Comic
Mrs. Dandywine: a self-aggrandizing matron, 50s

Here, Mrs. Dandywine describes herself to a guest.

MRS. DANDYWINE: Fortunately that will be no hindrance. I do not require people to listen and answers to my questions annoy me. There was a time when I read the newspapers with great alacrity; especially the obituaries. But hardly anyone of any interest is dying anymore. Miss Companion, you will make me one of what Mr. Orfington is drinking and refill his glass. You have heard of our mysterious knocking? It is a great comfort to me. Do you know my history? (…)
(Leans back in her chair, closes her eyes and after a proper interval begins to recite.) My history is my only passion. I was not, of course, born here. I was born away. No one was born here. To speak of. I remember great arguments among my relatives over my father's demise. Or rather over the money he left at his demise. My grandfather had been in the war and was killed when an automobile backfired outside the house on his ninetieth birthday. He mistook the explosion for gunfire, took cover in the hallway and was crushed by the fall of the clock. However, it was his clock. But that clock never ran after that. *(Pause.)* I remember great joy over a number of things I can't remember. There was a sense of eminent accomplishment and a time of confusion. I was of course proud enough to remain apart from personal contacts. I have always prided myself on my pride.

Vital Signs
Jane Martin
1990

Scene: here and now

Serio-Comic
Actress

Here the actress tells a sad tale about a pet iguana.

ACTRESS: I had me a pet iguana. Silver, green. Tied a red bow on him
'cause he moved fast. Kept in the shadows. Bought him at an
outdoor art fair. Halloween present. My brother's wife wouldn't
have him in the house. I didn't mind. Fed him a regular line of
flies. He was voracious. I started datin' this guard dog trainer
was a Viet Name vet. Real nice and reserved. Met him out to
the fairgrounds at the Fish and Game show. Had forearms big
as my waist. Wore a shoulder holster. Even in bed. We'd put on
Grateful Dead tapes, drink piña coladas, fool around all day. Sat
bolt upright in the Pullman bed, "Oh, oh," he says,"Incoming,"
he yells. Pulls a .45. "Infiltrators!" His eyes was all pupil. Nostrils
flared. "You ain't cuttin' off my balls." Starts firin'. I flattened
back on the head board. Used up the clip. There was holes in
the trailer and iguana on every flat surface in the room. "I think
you got him," I said. "Fucking Cong," he says. Fell back, slept
fourteen hours. I never tried to replace the iguana. There are
just certain things you shouldn't own because of the way the
world is. Certain things you shouldn't do either, but I'm not gettin' into that.

Arden of Feversham

Anonymous
1592

Scene: rural England

Serio-Comic
Black Will: a murderer, 30–50

Here, a thug brags of his various misdeeds.

WILL: Thou knowest, Greene, that I have lived in London this twelve
years, where I have made some go upon wooden legs for taking the wall on me; divers with silver noses for saying "There
goes Black Will!" I have cracked as many blades as thou hast
nuts. (…)
Faith, in a manner I have. The bawdy-houses have paid me trib-
ute; there durst not a whore set up, unless she have agreed
with me first for opening her shop-windows. For a cross word
of a tapster I have pierced one barrel after another with my
dagger, and held him by the ears till all his beer hath run out. In
Thames Street a brewer's cart was like to have run over me: I
made no more ado, but went to the clerk and cut all the notch-
es of his tallies, and beat them about his head. I and my company have taken the constable from his watch, and carried him
about the fields on a coltstaff. I have broken a sergeant's head
with his own mace, and bailed whom I list with my sword and
buckler. All the ten-penny-alehouses-men would stand every
morning with a quart-pot in their hand, saying, "Will it please
your worship drink?" He that had not done so, had been sure
to have had his sign pulled down and his lattice borne away the
next night. To conclude, what have I not done? yet cannot do
this; doubtless, he is preserved by miracle.

Dr. Faustus

Christopher Marlowe
Circa 1592

Scene: the study of Dr. Faustus

Dramatic
Faustus: a necromancer, 30s

Faustus has summoned the powerful Mephistopheles from Hell, who has agreed to do his bidding. Here, the foolish necromancer rejoices his dark accomplishment.

FAUSTUS: Had I as many souls as there be stars,
　　I'd give them all for Mephistophilis.
　　By him I'll be great Emperor of the world,
　　And make a bridge through the moving air,
　　To pass the ocean with a band of men;
　　I'll join the hills that bind the Afric shore,
　　And make that country continent to Spain,
　　And both contributory to my crown:
　　The Emperor shall not live but by my leave,
　　Nor any potentate of Germany.
　　Now that I have obtain'd what I desir'd,
　　I'll live in speculation of this art,
　　Till Mephistophilis return again.

Friar Bacon and Friar Bungay

Robert Greene
Circa 1589

Scene: England under the reign of Henry III

Serio-Comic
Lacy: the Earl of Lincoln, 20s

Lacy has fallen in love with Margaret, the keeper's daughter. Here, he contemplates marrying her.

LACY: Daphne, the damsel that caught Phoebus fast,
    And locked him in the brightness of her looks,
    Was not so beauteous in Apollo's eyes
    As is fair Margaret to the Lincoln Earl.
    Recant thee, Lacy, thou art put in trust.
    Edward, thy sovereign's son, hath chosen thee,
    A secret friend, to court her for himself,
    And dar'st thou wrong thy prince with treachery?
    Lacy, love makes no exception of a friend,
    Nor deems it of a prince but as a man.
    Honor bids thee control him in his lust;
    His wooing is not for to wed the girl,
    But to entrap her and beguile the lass.
    Lacy, thou lov'st, then brook not such abuse,
    But wed her, and abide thy prince's frown;
    For better die than see her live disgraced.

Friar Bacon and Friar Bungay

Robert Greene
Circa 1589

Scene: England under the reign of Henry III

Serio-Comic
Prince Edward: 20–30

When his best friend, the Earl of Lincoln, reveals that he plans to wed Margaret, a woman the prince also desires, the royal heir vows to woo her for himself.

PRINCE EDWARD: I tell thee, Peggy, I will have thy loves;
   Edward or none shall conquer Margaret.
   In frigates bottomed with rich Sethin planks,
   Topt with the lofty firs of Lebanon,
   Stemmed and incased with burnished ivory,
   And over-laid with plates of Persian wealth,
   Like Thetis shalt thou wanton on the waves,
   And draw the dolphins to thy lovely eyes,
   To dance lavoltas in the purple streams;
   Sirens, with harps and silver psalteries,
   Shall wait with music at thy frigate's stem,
   And entertain fair Margaret with their lays.
   England and England's wealth shall wait on thee;
   Britain shall bend unto her prince's love,
   And do due homage to thine excellence,
   If thou wilt be but Edward's Margaret.

Herod the Great

The Wakefield Pageant
Circa 1470

Scene: the court of Herod

Dramatic
Herod: King of Judea, 50–60

*When his advisors warm him of Isaiah's prophecy that a
child born to a virgin will become the Emmanuel, the
despot flies into a rage.*

HEROD: Why, and should I to him cower?
    Nay, there thou liest lightly!
    Fie! the devil thee speed, and me, but I drink once!
    This hast thou done, indeed, to anger me for the nonce;
    And thou, knave, thou thy meed shall have, by Cock's dear bones!
    Thou canst not half thy creed! Out, thieves, from my wones!
    Fie, knaves!
    Fie, dottypolls, with your books:
    Go cast them in the brooks!
    With such wiles and crooks
    My wit away raves.
    Heard I never such a trant, that a knave so slight
    Should come like a saint and reave me my right.
    Nay, he shall aslant; I shall kill him down straight.
    Ware! I say, let me pant. Now think I to fight
    For anger.
    My guts will out-thring
    But I this lad hang;
    Without I have avenging
    I may live no longer.
    Should a carl in a cave but of one year of age
    Thus make me to rave?

The Spanish Tragedy

Thomas Kyd
Circa 1586

Scene: Spain

Dramatic
Hieronimo: Marshall of Spain, 50s

Hieronimo's son, Horatio, has been found murdered in the royal palace. Here, the grieving father vows to avenge his death.

HIERONIMO: O eyes! no eyes, but fountains fraught with tears;
　　O life! no life, but lively form of death;
　　O world! no world, but mass of public wrongs,
　　Confused and filled with murder and misdeeds.
　　O sacred heavens! if this unhallowed deed,
　　If this unhuman and barbarous attempt,
　　If this incomparable murder thus
　　Of mine, but now no more my son,
　　Shall unrevealed and unrevengèd pass,
　　How should we term your dealings to be just,
　　If you unjustly deal with those that in your justice trust?
　　The night, sad secretary to my moans,
　　With direful visions wakes my vexèd soul,
　　And with the wounds of my distressful son
　　Solicits me for notice of his death.
　　The ugly fiends do sally forth of hell,
　　And frame my steps to unfrequented paths,
　　And fear my heart with fierce inflamèd thoughts.
　　The cloudy day my discontents records,
　　Early begins to register my dreams
　　And drive me forth to seek the murderer.
　　Eyes, life, world, heavens, hell, night and day,
　　See, search, show, send some man, some mean, that may—

A Chaste Maid in Cheapside

Thomas Middleton

Circa 1613

Scene: England

Serio-Comic
Tim: a bookwormish young man, 20s

Tim's marriage has been arranged by his overbearing parents. As he prepares to meet his bride-to-be, he laments his fate.

TIM: I mar'l what this gentlewoman should be
That I should have in marriage, she's a stranger to me:
I wonder what my parents mean i'faith,
To match me with a stranger so:
A maid that's neither kiff nor kin to me:
Life do they think I have no more care of my body,
Than to lie with one that I ne'er knew,
A mere stranger,
One that ne'er went to school with me neither,
Nor ever playfellows together?
They're mightily o'erseen in't methinks;
They say she has mountains to her marriage,
She's full of cattle, some two thousand runts;
Now what the meaning of these runts should be,
My tutor cannot tell me;
I have looked in Rider's dictionary for the letter R,
And there I can hear no tidings of these runts neither;
Unless they should be Rumford hogs,
I know them not,
And here she comes.
If I know what to say to her now
In the way of marriage, I'm no graduate;
Methinks i'faith 'tis boldly done of her
To come into my chamber being but a stranger;
She shall not say I'm so proud yet, but I'll speak to her:
Marry as I will order it,

She shall take no hold of my words I'll warrant her;
She looks and makes a curtsey—
Salve tu quoque puella pulcherrima,
Quid vis nescio nec sane curo—
Tully's own phrase to a heart.

A Chaste Maid in Cheapside

Thomas Middleton
Circa 1613

Scene: England

Dramatic
Sir Walter: a man whose debauched lifestyle has brought
him to ruin, 30–40

*His desire for the chaste young Moll has driven Sir Walter to
commit desperate crimes. Here, he teeters on the edge of
madness as he contemplates the base nature of his life.*

SIR WALTER: O my vengeance,
    Let me for ever hide my cursed face
    From sight of those, that darkens all my hopes,
    And stands between me and the sight of Heaven;
    Who sees me now, he too and those so near me,
    May rightly say, I am o'er-grown with sin;
    O how my offences wrestle with my repentance,
    It hath scarce breath—
    Still my adulterous guilt hovers aloft,
    And with her black wings beats down all my prayers
    Ere they be half way up; what's he knows now
    How long I have to live? O what comes then?
    My taste grows bitter, the round world, all gall now,
    Her pleasing pleasures now hath poisoned me,
    Which I exchanged my soul for;
    Make way a hundred sighs at once for me.

The Alchemist

Ben Jonson
1610

Scene: London

Serio-Comic
Subtle: a quack and con-man, 30–40

*Here, the clever Subtle describes his plan to con Sir Epicure
Mammon, by making the foolish man believe that he has a
magical stone that will cure all disease.*

SUBTLE: O, I did look for him
 With the sun's rising: marvel he could sleep!
 This is the day I am to perfect for him
 The *magisterium,* our great work, the stone;
 And yield it, made, into his hands, of which
 He has, this month, talked as he were possessed.
 And now he's dealing pieces on't away.
 Methinks I see him entering ordinaries,
 Dispensing for the pox, and plaguy houses,
 Reaching his dose, walking Moorfields for lepers,
 And offering citizens' wives pomander-bracelets,
 As his preservative, made of the elixir;
 Searching the spittle, to make old bawds young,
 And the highways, for beggars, to make rich;
 I see no end of his labors. He will make
 Nature ashamed of her long sleep, when art,
 Who's but a stepdame, shall do more than she,
 In her best love to mankind, ever could.
 If his dream last, he'll turn the age to gold.

The Alchemist

Ben Jonson
1610

Scene: London

Serio-Comic
Sir Epicure Mammon: a foolish nobleman, 40–50

*Sir Epicure Mammon has been conned by Subtle into
believing that he possesses a stone that can cure all disease.
Here, the greedy Mammon describes the financial and
social benefits of owning such a wondrous rock.*

MAMMON: Come on, sir. Now, you set your foot on shore
  In *Novo Orbe;* here's the rich Peru;
  And there within, sir, are the golden mines,
  Great Solomon's Ophir! he was sailing to't,
  Three years, but we have reached it in ten months.
  This is the day, wherein, to all my friends,
  I will pronounce the happy word, *be rich;*
  This day you shall be *spectatissimi.*
  You shall no more deal with the hollow die
  Or the frail card. No more be at charge of keeping
  The livery-punk for the young heir, that must
  Seal, at all hours, in his shirt. No more,
  If he deny, have him beaten to't, as he is
  That brings him the commodity. No more
  Shall thirst of satin, or the covetous hunger
  Of velvet entrails for a rude-spun cloak,
  To be displayed at Madam Augusta's, make
  The sons of Sword and Hazard fall before
  The golden calf, and on their knees, whole nights,
  Commit idolatry with wine and trumpets,
  Or go a feasting after drum and ensign.
  No more of this. You shall start up young viceroys,
  And have your punks, and punketees, my Surly.
  And unto thee I speak it first, *be rich.*

All for Love; or the World Well Lost

John Dryden
1677

Scene: Alexandria, 30 BC

Dramatic
Serapion: a priest of Isis, 40–60

Here, Cleopatra's priest recounts omens and portents which foreshadow the tragedy of Marc Antony's defeat and the final subjugation of Egypt.

SERAPION: In a lone aisle o' th' temple while I walked,
A whirlwind rose, that, with a violent blast,
Shook all the dome: the doors around me clapt;
The iron wicket, that defends the vault,
Where the long race of Ptolemies is laid,
Burst open, and disclosed the mighty dead.
From out each monument, in order placed,
An armèd ghost, start up: the boy-king last
Reared his inglorious head. A peal of groans
Then followed, and a lamentable voice
Cried, "Egypt is no more!' My blood ran back,
My shaking knees against each other knocked;
On the cold pavement down I fell entranced,
And so unfinished left the horrid scene.

All for Love; or the World Well Lost

John Dryden
1677

Scene: Alexandria, 30 BC

Dramatic
Marc Antony: General of Rome exiled in Alexandria, 40s

*As vengeful Caesar prepares to take Alexandria, history's
two most famous lovers prepare to die together. Here,
Antony speaks his final words to Cleopatra.*

MARC ANTONY: Enough: my life's not long enough for more.
　　Thou say'st thou wilt come after: I believe thee;
　　For I can now believe whate'er thou say'st
　　That we may part more kindly. (…)
　　But grieve not, while thou stay'st[,]
　　My last disastrous times:
　　Think we have had a clear and glorious day,
　　And heav'n did kindly to delay the storm,
　　Just till our close of ev'ning. Ten years' love,
　　And not a moment lost, but all improved
　　To th' utmost joys,—what ages have we lived!
　　And now to die each other's; and, so dying,
　　While hand in hand we walk in groves below,
　　Whole troops of lovers' ghosts shall flock about us,
　　And all the train be ours. (…)
　　No, not a minute.—This one kiss—more worth
　　Than all I leave to Caesar.

The Doctor in Spite of Himself

Moliere
1666

Scene: rural France

Serio-Comic
Sganarelle: a woodcutter-turned-physician, 30–40

Sganarelle has been forced to masquerade as a doctor by his avaricious wife. Here, he explains his predicament to a prospective client.

SGANARELLE: Devil take me if I know anything about medicine! You're a good sort, and I'm willing to confide in you, just as you are confiding in me. (…)
No, I tell you: they made me a doctor in spite of me. I had never bothered my head about being that learned; and all my studies went only up to seventh grade. I don't know what put this idea into their heads; but when I saw that they absolutely insisted on my being a doctor, I decided to be one, at the expense of whom it may concern. However, you'd never believe how the mistaken idea has gotten around, and how everybody is hell-bent on thinking me a learned man. They come looking for me from all directions; and if things keep on this way, I believe I'll stick to medicine all my life. I think it's the best trade of all; for whether you do well or badly, you're always paid just the same. Bad work never comes back onto our backs, and we cut the material we work on as we please. A cobbler making shoes could never botch a piece of leather without paying for the broken crockery; but in this work we can botch a man without its costing us anything. The blunders are never ours, and it's always the fault of the person who dies. In short, the best part of this profession is that there's a decency, an unparalleled discretion, among the dead; and you never see one of them complaining of the doctor who killed him.

The Doctor in Spite of Himself

Moliere
1666

Scene: rural France

Serio-Comic
Thibaut: a simple country lad, 20s

*Here, Thibaut tries to describe his mother's precarious
health to a physician.*

THIBAUT: She's sick of a proxy, sir. (…)
Yes, that is to say she's all swelled up all over; and they say it's a
whole lot of seriosities she's got inside her, and that her liver,
her belly, or her spleen, whatever you want to call it, 'stead of
making blood don't make nothing but water. Every other day
she has a quotigian fever, with pains and lassitules in the
muskles of her legs. You can hear in her throat phleg-ums like
to choke her; and sometimes she gets tooken with syncopations
and compulsions till I think she done passed away. In our village
we got a 'pothecary, all respect to him, who's given her I don't
know how many kinds of stuff; and it costs me more'n a dozen
good crowns in enemas, no offense, and beverages he had her
take, in jacinth confusions and cordial portions. But all that
stuff, like the feller said, was just a kind of salve that didn't
make her no better nor no worse. He wanted to slip her one
certain drug that they call hermetic wine; but me, frankly, I got
scared that would send her to join her ancestors; and they do
say those big doctors are killing off I don't know how many
people with that there invention.

The Innocent Mistress
Mary Pix
1697

Scene: London

Serio-Comic
Sir Francis Wildlove: a man about town, 20–30

Here, Sir Francis shares his thoughts on women.

SIR FRANCIS: As for the damosels, three sorts make a bushel, and will
be uppermost. First, there's your common jilts will oblige everybody. (…)
You may call 'em what you please, but they are very plentiful, I
promise you. The next is your kept mistress, she's a degree mod-
ester, if not kind to each, appears in her dress like quality, whilst
her ogling eyes, and too frequent debauches discovers her the
younger sister only to the first. (…)
The third is not a whore, but a brisk, airy, noisy coquette, that
lives upon treating. One spark has her to the play, another to
the park, a third to Windsor, a fourth to some other place of
diversion. She has not the heart to grant 'em all favours, for
that's their design at the bottom of the treats, and they have
not the heart to marry her, for that's her design, too, poor creature. So perhaps a year, or it may be two, the gaudy butterfly
flutters round the kingdom, then if a foolish cit does not take
compassion, sneaks into a corner, dies an old maid, despised
and forgotten. The men that fit those ladies are your rake, your
cully, and your beau. (…)
Gad, honest, honourable Ned, I must own I have a fling at all.
Sometimes I think it worth my while to make a keeper jealous;
frequently treat the coquette, till either she grows upon me, or I
grow weary of her. Then 'tis but saying a rude thing, she quarrels, I fly to the next bottle, and there forever drown her
remembrance.

The Learned Women

Moliere
1672

Scene: Paris

Serio-Comic
Clitandre: a young man in lust, 20s

Clitandre first proposed to scholarly Armande, who scorned his passion and demanded that he turn his vulgar urges of the flesh into something spiritual. Two years later, the greatly frustrated Clitandre gives up on Armande and proposes instead to her younger sister. When Armande angrily confronts him with his inability to attain a state of "perfect love" for her, he offers the following response.

CLITANDRE: Alas, Madame, with no offense to you
    I have a soul, but I've a body too;
    It sticks too closely to be set apart:
    Of such dismemberings I lack the art.
    Heaven has denied me that philosophy,
    And soul and body walk abreast with me.
    Nothing could be more beautiful, I own,
    Than purified desire for mind alone,
    Unions of hearts, the tender innocence
    Of thoughts completely undefiled by sense.
    And yet such loves for me are too refined;
    I am a trifle earthily inclined;
    When I'm in love, it's with a love entire
    For the whole person to whom I aspire.
    That's not a matter for great punishments,
    And—no offense to your fine sentiments—
    The world acknowledges my kind of passion,
    And marriage is sufficiently in fashion,
    Is thought a sweet, good enough way of life
    To have made me want to have you as my wife
    Without the liberty of such a notion
    Giving offense or causing such commotion.

The Lucky Chance
Aphra Behn
1686

Scene: London

Serio-Comic
Gayman: a spark of the town, 20–30

When Gayman receives a mysterious invitation to meet with an unknown woman promising love and fortune, the destitute charmer considers his options.

GAYMAN: Hum, I am awake, sure, and this is gold I grasp.
    I could not see this devil's cloven foot;
    Nor am I such a coxcomb to believe
    But he was as substantial as his gold.
    Spirits, ghosts, hobgoblins, furies, fiends and devils,
    I've often heard old wives fright fools and children with,
    Which, once arrived to common sense, they laugh at.
    No, I am for things possible and natural:
    Some female devil, old and damned to ugliness,
    And past all hopes of courtship and address,
    Full of another devil called desire,
    Has seen this face, this shape, this youth,
    And thinks it's worth her hire. It must be so.
    I must moil on in the damned dirty road,
    And sure, such pay will make the journey easy,
    And for the price of the dull, drudging night,
    All day I'll purchase new and fresh delight.

The Plain Dealer
William Wycherley
1676

Scene: London

Dramatic
Manly: a sea captain in love, 20s

Manly has returned from sea and is courting Olivia. When asked why he believes in her professed love for him, he offers the following explanation.

MANLY: I should, I confess, doubt the love of any other woman but her, as I do the friendship of any other man but him I have trusted; but I have such proofs of their faith as cannot deceive me. (...)

Not but I know that generally no man can be a great enemy but under the name of friend; and if you are a cuckold, it is your friend only that makes you so, for your enemy is not admitted to your house: if you are cheated in your fortune, 'tis your friend that does it, for your enemy is not made your trustee: if your honor or good name be injured, 'tis your friend that does it still, because your enemy is not believed against you. Therefore, I rather choose to go where honest, downright barbarity is professed, where men devour one another like generous, hungry lions and tigers, not like crocodiles; where they think the devil white, of our complexion; and I am already so far an Indian. But if your weak faith doubts this miracle of a woman, come along with me, and believe; and thou wilt find her so handsome that thou, who art so much my friend, wilt have a mind to lie with her, and so will not fail to discover what her faith and thine is to me.

When we're in love, the great adversity,
Our friends and mistresses at once we try.

The Relapse; or, Virtue in Danger

Sir John Vanbrugh
1696

Scene: Whitehall

Serio-Comic
Loveless: a married man struggling to observe his vows, 30s

Loveless has vowed to turn over a new leaf by remaining faithful to his wife, Amanda. Here, he tried desperately not to woo Amanda's cousin with whom he has become enamored.

LOVELESS: I'm satisfied. Now hear my symptoms,
And give me your advice. The first were these:
When 'twas my chance to see you at the play,
A random glance you threw, at first alarmed me;
I could not turn my eyes from whence the danger came:
I gazed upon you, till you shot again,
And then my fears came on me.
My heart began to pant, my limbs to tremble,
My blood grew thin, my pulse beat quick,
My eyes grew hot and dim, and all the frame
Of nature shook with apprehension.
'Tis true, some small recruits of resolution
My manhood brought to my assistance,
And by their help I made a stand a while,
But found at last your arrows flew so thick,
They could not fail to pierce me; so left the field,
And fled for shelter to Amanda's arms.
What think you of these symptoms, pray? (...)
Why, instantly she let me blood,
Which for the present much assuaged my flame.
But when I saw you, out it burst again,
And raged with greater fury than before.
Nay, since you now appear, 'tis so encreased
That in a moment, if you do not help me,
I shall, whilst you look on, consume to ashes.

The Rival Queens

Nathaniel Lee
1677

Scene: Babylon

Dramatic
Cassander: an angry young man in the court of Alexander
the great, 20s

*Alexander has taken Statira to be his second wife, thus
enraging Cassander. Here, the furious Cassander contemplates revolt.*

CASSANDER: The morning rises black, the low'ring sun,
    As if the dreadful business he foreknew,
    Drives heavily his sable chariot on.
    The face of day now blushes scarlet deep,
    As if it feared the stroke which I intend,
    Like that of Jupiter—lightning and thunder.
    The lords above are angry and talk big,
    Or rather walk the mighty cirque like mourners
    Clad in long clouds, the robes of thickest night,
    And seem to groan for Alexander's fall.
    'Tis as Cassander's soul could wish it were,
    Which, whensoe'er it flies at lofty mischief,
    Would startle fate and make all heav'n concerned.
    A mad Chaldean in the dead of night
    Came to my bedside with a flaming torch,
    And bellowing o'er me like a spirit damned,
    He cried, "Well had it been for Babylon
    If cursed Cassander never had been born."

The Sad Shepherd

Ben Jonson
1640

Scene: Sherwood

Dramatic
Eglamour: a sad shepherd, 20–30

Eglamour's beloved, Earine, had been reported drowned.
Here the grieving young man vows to somehow avenge her
death.

EGLAMOUR: If I could knit whole clouds about my brows,
 And weep like Swithin or those watery signs,
 The Kids that rise then, and drown all the flocks
 Of those rich shepherds dwelling in this vale,
 Those careless shepherds that did let her drown,
 Then I did something; or could make old Trent
 Drunk with my sorrow, to start out in breaches
 To drown their herds, their cattle, and their corn,
 Break down their mills, their dams, o'erturn their weirs,
 And see their houses and whole livelihood
 Wrought into water with her, all were good—
 I'd kiss the torrent and those whirls of Trent
 That sucked her in, my sweet Earine!
 When they have cast her body on the shore,
 And it comes up as tainted as themselves,
 All pale and bloodless, I will love it still,
 For all that they can do, and make them mad
 To see how I will hug it in mine arms,
 And hang upon the looks, dwell on her eyes,
 Feed round about her lips, and eat her kisses,
 Suck of her drownéd flesh!—and where's their malice?
 Not all their envious sousing can change that.
 But I will study some revenge past this!
 I pray you, give me leave, for I will study,
 Though all the bells, pipes, tabors, tambourines ring,
 That you can plant about me; I will study.

The Sad Shepherd

Ben Jonson
1640

Scene: Sherwood

Dramatic
Eglamour: a sad shepherd, 20–30

Here, Eglamour tells his friend, Robin Hood, that he can no longer enjoy the springtime.

EGLAMOUR: A spring, now she is dead! Of what? Of thorns?
    Briars and brambles? Thistles? Burrs and docks?
    Cold hemlock? Yew? The mandrake or the box?
    These may grow still; but what can spring beside?
    Did not the whole earth sicken when she died?
    As if there since did fall one drop of dew
    But what was wept for her, or any stalk
    Did bear a flower, or any branch a bloom,
    After her wreath was made! In faith, in faith,
    You do not fair to put these things upon me,
    Which can in no sort be. Earine,
    Who had her very being and her name
    With the first knots or buddings of the spring,
    Born with the primrose and the violet,
    Or earliest roses blown, when Cupid smiled,
    And Venus led the Graces out to dance,
    And all the flowers and sweets in nature's lap
    Leaped out, and made their solemn conjuration
    To last but while she lived! Do not I know
    How the vale withered the same day, how Dove,
    Dean, Eye, and Erwash, Idel, Snite, and Soare
    Each broke his urn, and twenty waters more
    That swelled proud Trent shrunk themselves dry? That, since,
    No sun or moon or other cheerful star
    Looked out of heaven, but all the cope was dark,
    As it were hung so for her exequies!
    And not a voice or sound to ring her knell

But of that dismal pair, the scritching owl
And buzzing hornet! Hark, hark, hark, the foul
Bird! How she flutters with her wicker wings!
Peace! You shall hear her scritch.

Tartuffe

Moliere
1644

Scene: 17th century Paris

Dramatic
Cleante: a man trying to help his brother, 30–60

Cleante is the exasperated brother of Orgon, a man who has allowed himself to be ruined by the scheming Tartuffe. When Orgon finally sees the errors of his ways, he flies into a belated rage. Here, Cleante chides his foolish brother for his extreme ways.

CLEANTE: Ah, there you go—extravagant as ever!
    Why can you not be rational? You never
    Manage to take the middle course, it seems,
    But jump, instead, between absurd extremes.
    You've recognized your recent grave mistake
    In falling victim to a pious fake;
    Now, to correct that error, must you embrace
    An even greater error in its place,
    And judge our worthy neighbors as a whole
    By what you've learned of one corrupted soul?
    Come, just because one rascal made you swallow
    A show of zeal which turned out to be hollow,
    Shall you conclude that all men are deceivers,
    And that, today, there are no true believers?
    Let atheists make that foolish inference;
    Learn to distinguish virtue from pretense,
    Be cautious in bestowing admiration,
    And cultivate a sober moderation.
    Don't humor fraud, but also don't asperse
    True piety; the latter fault is worse,
    And it is best to err, if err one must,
    As you have done, upon the side of trust.

The Tragedy of Sophonisba

John Marston
1606

Scene: Libya, the second Punic War

Dramatic
Gelosso: a senator from Carthage, 50–60

Sophonisba has nobly offered herself to Syphax to save her
beloved Carthage from being destroyed by his armies. Here,
wise old Gelosso praises her bravery but fears the final out-
come of her rash decision.

GELOSSO: A prodigy! Let Nature run cross-legged,
    Ops go upon her head, let Neptune burn,
    Cold Saturn crack with heat, for now the world
    Hath seen a woman!
    Leap nimble lightning from Jove's ample shield
    And make at length an end! The proud hot breath
    Of thee, contemning greatness, the huge drought
    Of sole self-loving vast ambition,
    Th'unnatural scorching heat of all those lamps
    Thou rear'dst to yield a temperate fruitful heat,
    Relentless rage, whose heart hath not one drop
    Of human pity,—all, all loudly cry,
    'Thy brand, O Jove!' For know the world is dry.
    O let a general end save Carthage fame!
    When worlds do burn, unseen's a city's flame.
    Phoebus in me is great. Carthage must fall.
    Jove hates all vice, but vows' breach worst of all.

Volpone

Ben Jonson
1606

Scene: Venice

Serio-Comic
Volpone: a crafty nobleman, 50–60

Volpone and his devious servant, Mosca, have plotted together to exploit his unscrupulous associates by making them believe that he is near death and that each has been named as the sole heir to his fortune. After being paid a visit by the aging Corbaccio—a man whose greed exceeds his concern over his ailing body—Volpone offers the following observation on the effects of human disintegration.

VOLPONE: So many cares, so many maladies,
    So many fears attending an old age,
    Yea, death so often called on, as no wish
    Can be more frequent with them, their limbs faint,
    Their senses dull, their seeing, hearing, going,
    All dead before them; yea, their very teeth,
    Their instruments of eating, failing them:
    Yet this is reckoned life! nay, here was one,
    Is now gone home, that wishes to live longer!
    Feels not his gout, nor palsy; feigns himself
    Younger by scores of years, flatters his age
    With confident belying it, hopes he may,
    With charms, like Æson, have his youth restored;
    And with these thoughts so battens, as if fate
    Would be as easily cheated on, as he,
    And all turns air!

Volpone

Ben Jonson
1606

Scene: Venice

Serio-Comic
Volpone: a crafty nobleman, 50–60

*Here, the rascally Volpone attempts to seduce Celia, the
lovely young wife of a man who has offered her favors to
Volpone in hopes of becoming his sole heir.*

VOLPONE: 'Tis the beggar's virtue;
    If thou hast wisdom, hear me, Celia.
    Thy baths shall be the juice of gilly-flowers,
    Spirit of roses, and of violets,
    The milk of unicorns, and panthers' breath
    Gathered in bags, and mixed with Cretan wines.
    Our drink shall be preparéd gold and amber;
    Which we will take, until my roof whirl round
    With the vertigo: and my dwarf shall dance,
    My eunuch sing, my fool make up the antic,
    Whilst we, in changèd shapes, act Ovid's tales,
    Thou, like Europa now, and I like Jove,
    Then I like Mars, and thou like Erycine:
    So, of the rest, till we have quite run through,
    And wearied all the fables of the gods.
    Then will I have thee in more modern forms,
    Attiréd like some sprightly dame of France,
    Brave Tuscan lady, or proud Spanish beauty;
    Sometimes, unto the Persian Sophy's wife,
    Or the Grand Signor's mistress; and, for change,
    To one of our most artful courtesans,
    Or some quick Negro, or cold Russian;
    And I will meet thee in as many shapes:
    Where we may so transfuse our wandering souls
    Out at our lips, and score up sums of pleasures.

The Beggar's Opera

John Gay
1728

Scene: London

Serio-Comic
Macheath: a notorious jade and highwayman, 30s

When Macheath is arrested for having compromised Polly Peachum, he is taken to Newgate Prison to await his execution. Here, the unrepentant cad muses over his fate.

MACHEATH: To what a woeful plight have I brought myself! Here must I (all day long, till I am hanged) be confined to hear the reproaches of a wench who lays her ruin at my door. I am in the custody of her father, and to be sure, if he knows of the matter I shall have a fine time on't betwixt this and my execution.—But I promised the wench marriage.—What signifies a promise to a woman? does not man in marriage itself promise a hundred things that he never means to perform? Do all we can, women will believe us; for they look upon a promise as an excuse for following their own inclinations.—But here comes Lucy, and I cannot get from her. Would I were deaf!

The Careless Husband
Colley Cibber
1705

Scene: Windsor

Dramatic
Sir Charles: a wayward husband, 30s

The philandering Sir Charles has been discovered by his wife sleeping in the same room with a serving woman. When he realizes that he has been found in such an indelicate situation, he laments his careless ways.

SIR CHARLES: How now! *(Feeling the steinkirk upon his head.)* What's this? How came it here? *(Puts on his wig.)* Did not I see my wife wear this today?—Death! she can't have been here, sure! It could not be jealousy that brought her home—for my coming was accidental—so too, I fear, might hers. How careless have I been!—not to secure the door neither!—'twas foolish. It must be so: she certainly has seen me here sleeping with her woman. If so, how low an hypocrite to her must that sight have proved me!—the thought has made me despicable ev'n to myself. How mean a vice is lying! and how often have these empty pleasures lulled my honor and my conscience to a lethargy, while I grossly have abused her, poorly skulking behind a thousand falsehoods! Now I reflect, this has not been the first of her discoveries. How contemptible a figure must I have made to her! A crowd of recollected circumstances confirm me now, she has been long acquainted with my follies, and yet with what amazing prudence has she borne the secret pangs of injured love, and wore an everlasting smile to me! This asks a little thinking—something should be done. I'll see her instantly, and be resolved from her behavior.

The Careless Husband

Colley Cibber

1705

Scene: Windsor

Dramatic
Sir Charles: a wayward husband, 30s

Sir Charles doesn't appreciate his wife, as the following declaration illustrates.

SIR CHARLES: So! the day is come again. Life but rises to another stage, and the same dull journey is before us. How like children do we judge of happiness! When I was stinted in my fortune almost everything was a pleasure to me because, most things then being out of my reach, I had always the pleasure of hoping for 'em; now Fortune's in my hand she's as insipid as an old acquaintance. It's mighty silly, faith. Just the same thing by my wife too; I am told she's extremely handsome—nay, and have heard a great many people say she is certainly the best woman in the world—why I don't know but she may [be], yet I could never find that her person or good qualities gave me any concern. In my eye the woman has no more charms than her mother.

The Careless Husband

Colley Cibber
1705

Scene: Windsor

Dramatic
Sir Charles: a wayward husband, 30s

*When one of Sir Charles' many conquests threatens to
leave him, he declares that he no longer has the strength or
patience to keep women.*

SIR CHARLES: Why then, seriously, I say, I am of late grown so very lazy
in my pleasures that I had rather lose a woman than go through
the plague and trouble of having or keeping her; and to be
free, I have found so much even in my acquaintance with you,
whom I confess to be a mistress in the art of pleasing, that I am
from henceforth resolved to follow no diversion that rises above
the degree of an amusement; and that woman that expects I
should make her my business, why, like my business, is then in a
fair way of being forgot. When once she comes to reproach me
with vows, usage, and stuff, I had as lief hear her talk of bills,
bonds, and ejectments; her passion becomes as troublesome as
a lawsuit, and I would as soon converse with my solicitor. In
short, I shall never care sixpence for any woman that won't be
obedient.

The Castle Spectre

Matthew G. Lewis
1797

Scene: a castle

Dramatic
Hassan: a black slave, 20–40

*When Hassan and Saib discuss the romantic foibles of their
masters, Hassan is reminded of his own true love, lost to
him forever in Africa.*

HASSAN: [Did it?] Oh Saib! my heart once was gentle, once was
good! But sorrows have broken it, insults have made it hard! I
have been dragged from my native land, from a wife who was
every thing to me, to whom I was every thing! Twenty years
have elapsed since these Christians tore me away: they tram-
pled upon my heart, mocked my despair, and, when in frantic
terms I raved of Samba, [they] laughed, and wondered how a
negro's soul could feel! In that moment when the last point of
Africa faded from my view, when as I stood on the vessel's deck
I felt that all [on earth] I loved was to me lost for ever, in that
bitter moment did I banish humanity from my breast. I tore
from my arm the bracelet of Samba's hair, I gave to the sea the
precious token, and, while the high waves swift bore it from
me, vowed aloud endless hatred to mankind. "I have kept my
oath, I *will* keep it!"

The Castle Spectre

Matthew G. Lewis
1797

Scene: a castle

Dramatic
Hassan: a black slave, 20–40

Hassan has long plotted to avenge his kidnapping and enslavement by destroying the man responsible for his miserable life. When his plan nears completion, Hassan takes comfort from the imminent devastation of his master's life.

HASSAN: Yes, thou art sweet, Vengeance!—"Oh! how it joys me when the white man suffers!"—Yet weak are his pangs, compared to those I felt when torn from thy shores, O native Africa!—from thy bosom, my faithful Samba!—Ah! dost thou still exist, my wife?—"Has sorrow for my loss traced thy smooth brow with wrinkles!"—My boy too, whom on that morning when the man-hunters seized me, I left sleeping on thy bosom, say, Lives he yet?—"Does he ever speak of me?—Does he ask, 'Mother, describe to me my father; show me how the warrior looked?'"—Ha! has my bosom still room for thoughts so tender? Hence with them! Vengeance must posses it all!—"Oh! when I forget my wrongs, may I forget myself!—When I forbear to hate these Christians, God of my fathers! mayst thou hate me!"—Ha! Whence that light? A man moves this way with a lamp!—How cautiously he steals along!—He must be watched. This friendly column will shield me from his regards. Silence! He comes.

Cato

Joseph Addison
1713

Scene: the Governor's Palace of Utica, 46 BC

Dramatic
Cato: Roman statesman who defied Caesar, 40s

Cato has joined with Pompeii in his revolt against Caesar. When Pompeii is killed, Cato is faced with confronting Caesar's legions. After listening to his generals argue for both war and peace, conservative Cato calls for moderation.

CATO: Let us appear nor rash nor diffident:
    Immoderate valor swells into a fault,
    And fear, admitted into public councils,
    Betrays like treason. Let us shun 'em both.
    Father, I cannot see that our affairs
    Are grown thus desp'rate. We have bulwarks round us;
    Within our walls are troops enured to toil
    In Afric's heats, and seasoned to the sun;
    Numidia's spacious kingdom lies behind us,
    Ready to rise at its young prince's call.
    While there is hope, do not distrust the gods;
    But wait at least till Caesar's near approach
    Force us to yield. 'Twill never be too late
    To sue for chains and own a conqueror.
    Why should Rome fall a moment ere her time?
    No, let us draw her term of freedom out
    In its full length, and spin it to the last,
    So shall we gain still one day's liberty;
    And let me perish, but in Cato's judgment,
    A day, an hour, of virtuous liberty
    Is worth a whole eternity in bondage.

Cato

Joseph Addison
1713

Scene: the Governor's Palace of Utica, 46 BC

Dramatic
Cato: Roman statesman who defied Caesar, 40s

When Decius tries to persuade Cato to make peace with Caesar, the renegade statesman describes his contempt for the emperor.

CATO: Let him consider that who drives us hither:
    'Tis Caesar's sword has made Rome's senate little,
    And thinn'd its ranks. Alas! thy dazzled eye
    Beholds this man in a false glaring light,
    Which conquest and success have thrown upon him;
    Didst thou but view him right, thou'dst see him black
    With murder, treason, sacrilege, and crimes
    That strike my soul with horror but to name 'em.
    I know thou look'st on me, as on a wretch
    Beset with ills, and covered with misfortunes;
    But, by the gods I swear, millions of worlds
    Should never buy me to be like that Caesar.

The Group

Mercy Otis Warren
1775

Scene: Massachusetts during the American Revolution

Dramatic
Monsieur: a man considering joining a group of Tories, 30s

The monsieur is torn between his desire for a title and memories of his father's tales of escaping a life of oppression in France as he here describes to a group of Tories.

MONSIEUR: Could I give up the dread of retribution,
    The awful reckoning of some future day,
    Like surly Hateall I might curse mankind,
    And dare the threatened vengeance of the skies.
    Or like yon apostate—*(Pointing to Hazelrod.)*
    Feel but slight remorse
    To sell my country for a grasp of gold.
    But the impressions of my early youth,
    Infixed by precepts of my pious sire,
    Are stings and scorpions in my goaded breast.
    Oft have I hung upon my parent's knee
    And heard him tell of his escape from France;
    He left the land of slaves and wooden shoes;
    From place to place he sought a safe retreat,
    Till fair Bostonia stretched her friendly arm
    And gave the refugee both bread and peace.
    (Shall I ungrateful 'rase the sacred bonds,
    And help to clank the tyrant's iron chains
    O'er these blest shores—once the sure asylum
    From all the ills of arbitrary sway?)
    With his expiring breath he bade his sons,
    If e'er oppression reached the western world,
    Resist its force, and break the servile yoke.

The Group

Mercy Otis Warren

1775

Scene: Massachusetts during the American Revolution

Dramatic
Hazelrod: a Judge who presides over a group of Tories, 50–60

Here, the passionate Hazelrod reacts to a fellow conspirator's call for moderation.

HAZELROD: This balancing of passions ne'er will do,
And by the scale which virtue holds to reason,
Weighing the business ere he executes,
Doubting, deliberating, half resolved
To be the savior of a virtuous state,
Instead of guarding refugees and knaves,
The buzzing reptiles that crawl round his court,
And lick his hand for some delicious crumb
Or painted plume to grace the guilty brow,
Stained with ten thousand falsities, trumped up
To injure every good and virtuous name
Who won't strike hands and be his country's foe:
I'll hasten after, and stir up his soul
To dire revenge and bloody resolutions,
Or the whole fabric falls on which we hang,
And down the pit of infamy we plunge,
Without the spoils we long have hoped to reap.

The Jealous Wife

George Colman
1761

Scene: London

Serio-Comic
Major Oakly: a knowing bachelor, 30s

When his brother's marriage hits the rocks, this hind-sighted bachelor laments his sibling's inability to manage his life.

MAJOR OAKLY: Well said, William! No bad hint for me perhaps! What a strange world we live in! No two people in it love one another better than my brother and sister, and yet the bitterest enemies could not torment each other more heartily. Ah, if he had but half my spirit! And yet he don't want it neither. But I know his temper: he pieces out the matter with maxims, and scraps of philosophy, and odds and ends of sentences: 'I must live in peace'—'Patience is the best remedy'—'anything for a quiet life'—and so on! However, yesterday, to give him his due, he behaved like a man. Keep it up, brother! keep it up! or it's all over with you. Since mischief is on foot, I'll e'en set it forwards on all sides. I'll in to him directly, read him one of my morning-lectures, and persuade him, if I possibly can, to go out with me immediately; or work him up to some open act of rebellion against the sovereign authority of his lady-wife. Zounds, brother, rant, and roar, and rave, and turn the house out of the window. If I was a husband! S'death, what a pity it is that nobody knows how to manage a wife, but a bachelor.

Julia of Louvain; or, Monkish Cruelty

J.C. Cross

1797

Scene: Louvain, France

Dramatic
St. Pierre: a man obsessed with a woman who spurns his
love, 30s

*When the virtuous Julia announces that she'll join a convent
rather than marry him, the evil St. Pierre vows to destroy
her.*

ST. PIERRE: The tempest rages here! in vain
    I bid the storm depart;
    Ambition racks my tortur'd brain,
    And tyrant love my heart.
    Give to my arms the scornful maid,
    Tho' hatred be her dower;
    Or on the cold earth see her laid,
    The victim of my power!
    Thus, should the timid hare essay,
    T'escape the watchful tyger's eyes,
    He eager fastens on his prey,
    It faintly struggles, groans, and dies.

The Kentish Barons

Francis North
1791

Scene: Castle Mortimer

Dramatic
Mortimer: an evil and powerful lord, 40–50

Here Lord Mortimer ruminates on the tendency of men to deny their true natures.

MORTIMER: How disappointment loves to plague the heart
    Of that poor ideot man! who vainly thinks
    His reason given to direct and guide him.
    The happy brutes, who follow instinct's laws,
    Enjoy the blessings of the present hour:
    Their daily task perform'd, they lay them down,
    And never dream that the approaching morn
    Shall wake them to new labours. Man alone
    Looks through a flattering and deceitful glass,
    And vainly strives to view futurity:
    Nature has wisely hid it from his sight;
    Bur purblind Reason, curious and inquisitive,
    Just sees enough to dazzle and mislead him.

The Kentish Barons

Francis North
1791

Scene: Castle Mortimer

Dramatic
Osbert: an unhappy young man, 20s

*When Osbert, servant to the dread Mortimer, is ordered to
assist his lord in the seduction of the virtuous Elina, he
laments his inability to save Elina from Mortimer's clutches.*

OSBERT: Oh! ye soft spirits, who reside above,
And look with pity down on man's calamities,
Protect and guard me. Ah! what fault of mine,
What crime have I committed, that my fortune
Should urge me on to such a deed as this?
What can I do? O shameful! shameful Nature,
Why wilt thou plead for life, for guilty life,
Which proves a burthen to the wretch that bears it!
Yet who can, in the morning of his days,
Look, without trembling on the night of death?
[Darkness eternal Darkness! O my soul!
Recoils with horror at the dreary prospect,]
Ye powers, who take delight in innocence,
Direct me in the path I'm forc'd to tread;
Preserve my life, and save my youth from guilt!

The London Merchant; or, The History of George Barnwell

George Lillo
1731

Scene: London

Dramatic
George Barnwell: a young man driven to criminal acts by a scheming woman, 20s

George has allowed himself to fall under the spell of the duplicitous Millwood, who has convinced him to steal from his employer. Here, Barnwell contemplates his fall from grace.

GEORGE BARNWELL: How strange are all things round me! Like some thief, who treads forbidden ground and fain would lurk unseen, fearful I enter each apartment of this well-known house. To guilty love, as if that were too little, already have I added breach of trust.—A thief!—Can I know myself that wretched thing, and look my honest friend and injured master in the face? Though hypocrisy may a while conceal my guilt, at length it will be known, and public shame and ruin must ensue. In the meantime, what must be my life? Ever to speak a language foreign to my heart; hourly to add to the number of my crimes in order to conceal 'em! Sure, such was the condition of the grand apostate, when first he lost his purity; like me, disconsolate he wandered, and, while yet in heaven, bore all of his future hell about him.

The London Merchant; or,
The History of George Barnwell

George Lillo
1731

Scene: London

Dramatic
Uncle: a man with a keen sense of his own doom, 50–60

A man about to be murdered here has a dark premonition immediately prior to his demise.

UNCLE: If I were superstitious, I should fear some danger lurked unseen, or death were nigh. A heavy melancholy clouds my spirits; my imagination is filled with gashly forms of dreary graves and bodies changed by death, when the pale, lengthened visage attracts each weeping eye, and fills the musing soul, at once, with grief and horror, pity and aversion. I will indulge the thought. The wise man prepares himself for death by making it familiar to his mind. When strong reflections hold the mirror near, and the living in the dead behold their future selves, how does each inordinate passion and desire cease, or sicken at the view! The mind scarce moves; the blood, curdling and chilled, creeps slowly through the veins—fixed, still, and motionless we stand—so like the solemn object of our thoughts, we are almost at present—what we must be hereafter, till curiosity awakes the soul and sets it on inquiry. —O Death, thou strange mysterious power, seen every day, yet never understood but by the incommunicative dead, what art thou? The extensive mind of man, that with a thought circles the earth's vast globe, sinks to the center, or ascends above the stars; that worlds exotic finds, or thinks it finds—thy thick clouds attempts to pass in vain: lost and bewildered in the horrid gloom, defeated she returns more doubtful than before, of nothing certain—but of labor lost.

The London Merchant; or, The History of George Barnwell

George Lillo
1731

Scene: London

Dramatic
George Barnwell: a young man driven to criminal acts by a scheming woman, 20s

Millwood has convinced George to murder his uncle for money. Following the violent deed, Barnwell removes his mask and sobs over his uncle's body.

GEORGE BARNWELL: Expiring saint! O murdered, martyred uncle! Lift up your dying eyes, and view your nephew in your murderer! Oh, do not look so tenderly upon me! Let indignation lighten from your eyes, and blast me ere you die!—By heaven, he weeps in pity of my woes. Tears,—tears, for blood! The murdered, in the agonies of death, weeps for his murderer.—Oh, speak your pious purpose—pronounce my pardon then—and take me with you!—He would, but cannot.—Oh, why, with such fond affection, do you press my murdering hand?—What! will you kiss me? *(Barnwell kisses his uncle, who groans and dies.)* Life, that hovered on his lips but till he had sealed my pardon, in that kiss expired. He's gone forever—and oh! I follow. *(Swoons away upon his uncle's dead body.)* —Do I still live to press the suffering bosom of the earth? Do I still breathe, and taint with my infectious breath the wholesome air? Let heaven from its high throne, in justice or in mercy, now look down on that dear murdered saint and me the murderer, and, if his vengeance spares, let pity strike and end my wretched being!—Murder the worst of crimes, and parricide the worst of murders, and this the worst of parricides! Cain, who stands on record from the birth of time, and must to its last final period, as accursed, slew a brother favored above him. Detested Nero by another's hand dispatched a mother that he feared and hated. But I, with my own hand, have murdered a brother, mother, father, and a friend most loving and beloved. This execrable act of mine's without a parallel. Oh, may it ever stand alone—the last of murders, as it is the worst!

The Rivals

Richard Brinsley Sheridan
1775

Scene: Bath

Serio-Comic
Sir Anthony Adverse: an overbearing father, 50s

*When his son refuses to marry the young lady he has
selected, Sir Anthony angrily confronts him with his willful
disobedience. When the young man refuses to honor his
father's demands, Sir Anthony flies into a rage and threatens to disown him.*

SIR ANTHONY: None of your passion, sir! none of your violence! if you
please.—It won't do with me, I promise you. (…)
['Tis a confounded lie!]—I know you are in a passion in your
heart; I know you are, you hypocritical young dog! But it won't
do. (…)
[So you will fly out!] Can't you be cool, like me? What the devil
good can *passion* do!—*Passion* is of no service, you impudent,
insolent, overbearing reprobate!—There you sneer again!—
don't provoke me!—But you rely upon the mildness of my temper—you do, you dog! you play upon the meekness of my dis-
position! Yet take care—the patience of a saint may be over-
come at last!—but mark! I give you six hours and a half to consider of this: if you then agree, without any condition, to do
everything on earth that I choose, why—confound you! I may in
time forgive you—If not, z——ds! don't enter the same hemi-
sphere with me! don't dare to breathe the same air, or use the
same light with me; but get an atmosphere and a sun of your
own! I'll strip you of your commission; I'll lodge a five-and-
threepence in the hands of trustees, and you shall live on the
interest.—I'll disown you, I'll disinherit you, I'll unget you! and—
d—n me, if ever I call you Jack again!

The Rivals

Richard Brinsley Sheridan
1775

Scene: Bath

Dramatic
Faulkland: a man who has just lost the woman he loves,
20s

*Foolish Faulkland has allowed jealousy and poor judgment
to drive away Julia, his fiancee. When she finally declares
their engagement to be terminated, the young man
laments his loss.*

FAULKLAND: She's gone!—forever!—There was an awful resolution in
her manner, that riveted me to my place.—O fool!—dolt!—bar-
barian!—Curst as I am with more imperfections than my fellow-
wretches, kind Fortune sent a heaven-gifted cherub to my aid,
and, like a ruffian, I have driven her from my side!—I must now
haste to my appointment.—Well, my mind is tuned for such a
scene.—I shall wish only to become a principal in it, and reverse
the tale my cursed folly put me upon forging here.—O love!—
tormentor!—fiend! whose influence, like the moon's acting on
men of dull souls, makes idiots of them, but meeting subtler
spirits, betrays their course, and urges sensibility to madness!

The Tragedy of Jane Shore
Nicholas Rowe
1714

Scene: London, June 1483

Dramatic
Lord Hastings: a man torn between his love for Jane Shore
and his dark passion for the tempestuous Alicia, 20–30

*Following a particularly harrowing encounter with Alicia,
Hastings reflects upon her stormy nature as he prepares to
meet with calm and gentle Jane.*

LORD HASTINGS: How fierce a fiend is passion. With what wildness,
   What tyranny untamed, it reigns in woman.
   Unhappy sex! whose easy, yielding temper
   Gives way to every appetite alike;
   Each gust of inclination, uncontrolled,
   Sweeps through their souls and sets 'em in an uproar;
   Each motion of the heart rises to fury,
   And love in their weak bosoms is a rage
   As terrible as hate and as destructive.
   So the wind roars o'er the wide fenceless ocean,
   And heaves the billows of the boiling deep,
   Alike from north, from south, from east, from west;
   With equal force the tempest blows by turns
   From every corner of the seaman's compass.
   But soft ye now—for here comes one disclaims
   Strife and her wrangling train. Of equal elements,
   Without one jarring atom, was she formed,
   And gentleness and joy make up her being.

The Tragedy of Tragedies; or, The Life and Death of Tom Thumb The Great

Henry Fielding
1730/31

Scene: the Court of King Arthur, and a Plain thereabouts

Serio-Comic
Grizzle: a man who has lost the woman he loves to Tom Thumb, 20–30

When Princess Huncamunca marries Tom Thumb, her erstwhile suitor, Grizzle, flies into a vengeful rage.

GRIZZLE: Ha! dost thou own they falsehood to my face?
　　Think'st thou that I will share thy husband's place?
　　Since to that office one cannot suffice,
　　And since you scorn to dine one single dish on,
　　Go, get your husband put into commission.
　　Commissioners to discharge (ye gods! it fine is)
　　The duty of a husband to your Highness.
　　Yet think not long I will my rival bear,
　　Or unrevenged the slighted willow wear;
　　The gloomy, brooding tempest, now confined
　　Within the hollow caverns of my mind,
　　In dreadful whirl shall roll along the coasts,
　　Shall thin the land of all the men it boasts,
　　And cram up ev'ry chink of hell with ghosts,
　　So have I seen, in some dark winter's day,
　　A sudden storm rush down the sky's highway,
　　Sweep through the streets with terrible ding-dong,
　　Gush through the spouts, and wash whole crowds along.
　　The crowded shops the thronging vermin screen,
　　Together cram the dirty and the clean,
　　And not one shoe-boy in the street is seen.

The Way of the World
William Congreve
1700

Scene: London

Dramatic
Sir Wilfull Witwoud: a country gentleman preparing to travel abroad, 40

Before embarking on a journey for the purpose of improving himself, Sir Wilfull pays a visit to his aunt, Lady Wishfort, in whose home he encounters his estranged brother, Anthony, who has turned into a complete fop. Here, the rusticated Sir Wilfull lambastes Anthony for his foolish city ways.

SIR WILFULL: The fashion's a fool; and you're a fop, dear brother. 'Sheart, I've suspected this. By'r Lady, I conjectured you were a fop, since you began to change the style of your letters, and write in a scrap of paper gilt round the edges, no broader than a *subpoena*. I might expect this when you left off 'Honored Brother,' and 'hoping you are in good health,' and so forth—to begin with a 'Rat me, knight, I'm so sick of a last night's debauch'—Od's heart, and then tell a familiar tale of a cock and a bull, and a whore and a bottle, and so conclude. You could write news before you were out of your time, when you lived with honest Pumple Nose, the attorney of Furnival's Inn. You could intreat to be remembered then to your friends round the Wrekin. We could have gazettes then, and Dawks's Letter, and the weekly bill, 'till of late days.

The Witlings

Frances Burney
1780

Scene: London

Serio-Comic
Censor: a man of Sardonic sensibility, 30s

*Here, the jaded Censor chastises a friend for his inconsistent
behavior with his mistress.*

CENSOR: How gloriously inconsistent is the conduct of a professed
lover! while to his mistress he is all tame submission and abject
servility, to the rest of the world he is commanding, selfish, and
obstinate; everything is to give way to him, no convenience is to
be consulted, no objections are to be attended to in opposition
to his wishes. It seems as if he thought it the sole business of
the rest of mankind to study his single interest,—in order, perhaps to recompense him for pretending to his mistress that he
has no will but hers.

The Witlings

Frances Burney
1780

Scene: London

Serio-Comic
Dabbler: a man who fancies himself a poet, 30–40

When his work is interrupted, the pretentious Dabbler has a hard time regaining his train of thought.

DABBLER: What a provoking intrusion! just as I had worked myself into the true spirit of poetry!—I sha'n't recover my ideas this half hour. 'Tis a most barbarous thing that a man's retirement cannot be sacred. *(Sits down to write.)* Ye *fighting,*—no, that was not it,—ye ye—ye—O curse it, *(Stamping.)* if I have not forgot all I was going to say! That unfeeling, impenetrable fool has lost me more ideas than would have made a fresh man's reputation. I'd rather have given a hundred guineas than have seen her. I protest, I was upon the point of making as good a poem as any in the language,—my numbers flowed,—my thoughts were ready,—my words glided,—but now, all is gone!—all gone and evaporated! *(Claps his hand to his forehead.)* Here's nothing left! nothing in the world!—What shall I do to compose myself? Suppose I read?—why where the Deuce are all the things gone? *(Looking over his papers.)* O, here,—I wonder how my epigram will read today,—I think I'll show it to Censor,—he has seen nothing like it of late;—I'll pass it off for some dead poet's, or he'll never do it justice;—let's see, Suppose Pope?—No, it's too smart for Pope,—Pope never wrote anything like it!

Arms and the Man

George Bernard Shaw
1894

Scene: Bulgaria, 1885

Dramatic
Sergius: a young military officer, 20s

Sergius has recently returned from battle and is being hailed a brave hero. When asked by Louka, the servant girl he secretly loves, if he considers himself to be a brave man, he offers the following insight.

SERGIUS: They all slashed and cursed and yelled like heroes. Psha! the courage to rage and kill is cheap. I have an English bull terrier who has as much of that sort of courage as the whole Bulgarion nation, and the whole Russian nation at its back. But he lets my groom thrash him, all the same. That's your soldier all over! No, Louka: your poor men can cut throats; but they are afraid of their officers; they put up with insults and blows; they stand by and see one another punished like children: aye, and help to do it when they are ordered. And the officers!!! Well *(With a short harsh laugh.)* I am an officer. Oh, *(Fervently.)* give me the man who will defy to the death any power on earth or in heaven that sets itself up against his own will and conscience: he alone is the brave man.

The Bear

Anton Chekhov, Trans. by Carol Rocamora
1888

Scene: the drawing room of Popova's country estate, some-where in provincial Russia

Comedic
Grigory Stepanovich Smirnov: a landowner in his prime, 40s

When Smirnov arrives at the home of the recently widowed Helen to collect one of her late husband's debts, he becomes outraged when she refuses to pay. Here, he details his rather bleak opinion of the fairer sex.

SMIRNOV: *(Mimicking.)* 'Course and not very clever!' And 'I don't know how to conduct myself in female company!' Is that it?! My dear lady, I have seen more women in my time than you've seen sparrows! Three duels I have fought over women, I've spurned a dozen more, and nine others have spurned me! That's right! Oh, yes, there were times when I played the fool, when I whispered sweet nothings, uttered honeyed words, showered pearls of flattery, when I simpered and swooned...I loved, I suffered, I sighed at the moon, I pined, I languished, I wasted away, I blew hot and cold...I loved madly, passionately, every which way, God help me, I chattered like a magpie about emancipation, I squandered half my soul on the tender passion, and now, thank you very much, but no thank you! You beguile me no longer! Enough! *(Sings.)* "Ochi chornye, ochi strastnye," dark eyes, passionate glances, crimson lips, dimpled cheeks, timid sighs, moonlight, whispers—for all this, madam, I would-n't give a copper kopek! Present company excluded, of course, but all other women, great and small, they're all hypocrites, phonies, gossips, scandalmongers, haters, slanderers, liars to the marrow of their bones, they're petty, fussy, ruthless, they're absolutely illogical, and as for what they've got upstairs *(strikes his forehead)*, well, forgive me for saying so, but even a sparrow could outdo a philosopher if it's one who's wearing a skirt! Just take a look at one of these poetic creatures: a haze of muslin, an elixer of essence, a veritable goddess, but look deeper into her soul, and what do you see? Your every-day common crocodile! *(He siezes the back of a chair; it splinters and breaks.)* And what's so amazing about this crocodile is that for some reason she imagines that her masterpiece, her territory, her sacred domain—is the human heart! Curse me, hang me upside down by my heels, if a woman can love anyone more than a lapdog! …In love, she only can simper and snivel! While the man suffers and sacrifices, she only swirls her train and holds on tighter to his poor nose. You have the extreme misfortune of being a woman, you must know from personal experience all about feminine nature. Tell me the truth—have you ever in your life seen a woman who is capable of being honest, faithful and true? You haven't! The only honest and true ones are old maids and freaks! You'd see a horned cat or a white woodcock sooner than you would a faithful woman!

Black-Ey'd Susan

Douglas Jerrold
1829

Scene: a village by the sea

Dramatic
Jacob Twig: village bailiff, a toady, 20s

Jacob had been in the employ of the evil Doggrass for whom he has done much dirty work. An encounter with mortality has inspired the young man to change his life, as he here explains.

JACOB: Yes; I was in the public-house when the Captain was brought in with that gash in his shoulder; I stood beside his bed, it was steeped in blood—the doctor shook his head—the parson came and prayed; and when I looked on the Captain's blue lips and pale face, I thought what poor creatures we are; then something whispered in my heart, 'Jacob, thou hast been a mischief-making, wicked lad—and suppose, Jacob, thou wert, at a moment's notice, to take the Captain's place!' I heard this—heard it as plain as my own voice—and my hair moved, and I felt as if I'd been dipped in a river, and I fell like a stone on my knees—when I got up again, I was quite another lad.

Black-Ey'd Susan

Douglas Jerrold
1829

Scene: a village by the sea

Dramatic
William: a man about to be executed, 30s

*William, a sailor, has been away at sea for many months.
When he returns, he discovers his wife, Susan, being
seduced against her will by a senior officer, whom he
attacks. Sentenced to death for his crime, William here
meets for the first time with his beloved Susan, and makes
his final wish.*

WILLIAM: Susan, be calm. If you love your husband, do not send him
on the deck a white-faced coward. Be still my poor girl, I have
something to say—until you are calm, I will not utter it; now
Susan— (...)
Susan! you know the old aspen that grows near to the church
porch; you and I, when children, almost before we could speak
plainly, have sat and watched, and wondered at its shaking
leaves—I grew up, and that tree seemed to me a friend that
loved me, yet had not the tongue to tell me so. Beneath its
boughs our little arms have been locked together—beneath its
boughs I took the last kiss of your white lips when hard fortune
made me turn sailor. I cut from the tree this little branch.
(Produces it.) Many a summer's day aboard, I've lain in the top
and looked at these few leaves, until I saw green meadows in
the salt sea, and heard the bleating of the sheep. When I am
dead, Susan, let me be laid under that tree—let me—

De Monfort

Joanna Baillie

1800

Scene: a village in Germany

Dramatic
De Monfort: a man consumed with hatred and jealousy,
20–30

De Monfort has spent the better part of his life hating his childhood rival, Rezenvelt. When his enemy appears at his castle with the intent of marrying De Monfort's sister, he flies into a rage.

DE MONFORT: *(Alone, tossing his arms distractedly.)* Hell hath no greater torment for th'accurs'd
Than this man's presence gives—
Abhorred fiend! he hath a pleasure too,
A damned pleasure in the pain he gives!
"Oh! the side glance of that detested eye!"
That conscious smile! that full insulting lip!
It touches every nerve: "it makes me mad.
What, does it please thee? Dost thou woo my hate?
Hate shalt thou have! determin'd, deadly hate,
Which shall awake no smile." Malignant villain!
The venom of thy mind is rank and devilish,
And thin the film that hides it.
"Thy hateful visage ever spoke thy worth:
I loath'd thee when a boy."
That [men] should be besotted with him thus!
And Freberg likewise so bewitched is,
That like a hireling flatt'rer, at his heels
He meanly paces, off'ring brutish praise,
O! I could curse him too.

De Monfort

Joanna Baillie
1800

Scene: a village in Germany

Dramatic
De Monfort: a man consumed with hatred and jealousy,
20–30

Driven insane by his hatred for Rezenvelt, De Monfort follows his enemy into the woods with murder on his mind.

DE MONFORT: How hollow groans the earth beneath my tread!
    Is there an echo here? Methinks it sounds
    As tho' some heavy footstep follow'd me.
    "I will advance no farther.
    Deep settled shadows rest across the path,
    And thickly-tangled boughs o'er hang this spot.
    O that a tenfold gloom did cover it!
    That 'midst the murky darkness I might strike;
    As in the wild confusion of a dream,
    Things horrid, bloody, terrible, do pass,
    As tho' thy pass'd not; nor impress the mind
    With the fix'd clearness of reality."
    (An owl is heard screaming near him.)
    (Starting.) What sound is that? *(Listens, and owl cries again.)* It
    is the screech-owl's cry.
    Foul bird of night! what spirit guides thee here?
    Art thou instinctive drawn to scenes of horrour?
    "I've heard of this. *(Pauses and listens.)*"
    How those fall'n leaves so rustle on the path,
    With whisp'ring noise, as tho' the earth around me
    Did utter sweet things!
    The distant river, too, bears to mine ear
    A dismal wailing. O mysterious night!
    Thou art not silent; many tongues hast thou.
    A distant gath'ring blast sounds thro' the wood,
    And dark clouds fleetly hasten o'er the sky.

O! that a storm would rise, a raging storm;
Amidst the roar of warring elements
I'd lift my hand and strike: but this pale light,
The calm distinctness of each stilly thing,
Is terrible.

An Enemy of the People

Ibsen, Trans. by Brian Johnston and Rick Davis
1882

Scene: a coastal town in Southern Norway

Dramatic
Dr. Thomas Stockmann: a man crusading for truth, 30–40

Dr. Stockmann is the staff physician at the local mineral baths which provide the town with most of its income. When the baths are found to be contaminated, Stockmann orders them closed. He is out-voted by the people of the town, led by his brother, the mayor. Here, the idealistic doctor confronts the entire community with their stupidity.

DR. STOCKMANN: I say that the majority is never right! That's just one of those shibboleths that any free man capable of thinking must rebel against. Take any country—who makes up this majority? The intelligent people or the stupid ones? I think we can all agree that the stupid people are a terrifying, overwhelming majority anywhere in the world. But damn it, it can't be right that the stupid should hold power over the intelligent. (…) Yes, yes, you can shout me down, but you can't refute me. The majority has the power, unfortunately—but it doesn't possess the right. The right is with me and a few others, the lonely few. The minority is always in the right. (…) I've already said that I'm not going to waste my breath on that scrawny, short-winded pack of old has-beens. The beating pulse of life has already passed them by. No, I'm thinking about the few, the rare individuals, who've seen all the new truths springing up around us. These men stand at the outposts—so far in the vanguard that the solid majority hasn't even caught sight of them yet—and out there, they're fighting for truths too newly born into the world's consciousness for the majority to support. (…) You're damn right I am, Mr. Hovstad. I'm making a revolution against this lie that the majority has the truth on its side. What are these truths the majority rallies around? These truths are so decrepit with age that they're nearly senile. But, gentlemen, when a truth has grown so ancient, it's well on its way to becoming a lie.

The Family Legend

Joanna Baillie
1810

Scene: the Isle of Mull

Dramatic
John of Lorne: a warrior, 20s

John's sister and best friend have lost their chance for a life together because of clan warfare. Here, John confesses his love of war.

JOHN: A noble heart thou hast: such manly meekness
Becomes they generous nature. But for me,
More fierce and wilful, sorely was I chafed
To see thy faithful heart robbed of its hope,
All for the propping up a hollow peace
Between two warlike clans, who will, as long
As bagpipes sound, and blades flash to the sun,
Delighting in the noble sport of war,
Some fierce opponents find. What doth it boot,
If men in fields must fight, and blood be shed,
What clans are in the ceaseless strife opposed? (…)
The warlike minstrel's rousing lay thou lov'st:
Shall bards in the hall sing of our fathers' deeds
To lull their sons to sleep? Vain simple wish!
I love to hear the sound of holy bell,
And peaceful men their praises lift to heaven:
I love to see around their blazing fire
The peasant and his cheerful family set,
Eating their fearless meal. But, when the roar
Of battle rises, and the closing clans,
Darkening the sun-gleamed heath, in dread affray
Are mingled; blade with blade, and limb with limb,
Nerve-strained, in terrible strength; yea, soul with soul
Nobly contending; who would raise aloft
The interdicting hand, and say, 'Be stilled?'
If this in me be sin, may heaven forgive me!
That being am not I.

The Female Enthusiast

Sarah Pogson
1807

Scene: France during the Revolution

Dramatic
Belcour: a young man in love, 20s

*Virtuous Belcour has promised to help his best friend,
Henry, win the heart of the woman he loves, only to discover that the woman in question is his own beloved Estelle.*

BELCOUR: "Oh, Estelle!" What, Henry dote on Estelle?
    It cannot, must not be. Henry, I dote—
    All! All but this, of fortune and of fame,
    I could yield to thee! But Estelle never!
    She is entwined with every thought and nerve,
    And I could as soon change the course of day's
    Refulgent orb as remove from my hopes
    Their brightest object—my adored Estelle!
    Why did I not to Henry long ago
    Declare my intentions? But there is no blame
    Attaches to my silence, more than his.
    Alas! That hateful journey sealed my lips;
    Nor would I trust my pen. He was doubtless
    By the same cause restrained—our separation.
    And thus, while gaining trash to fill my purse,
    The nobler treasure of my heart is lost!

The Female Enthusiast

Sarah Pogson
1807

Scene: France during the Revolution

Dramatic
Marat: French politician and co-conspirator of Danton and Robespierre, 50s

Here, Marat addresses a ragged Parisian mob.

MARAT: Citizens! These difficulties shall cease,
    And the head of each base conspirator—
    Each foe to liberty and equality
    Shall roll beneath us, an abject football.
    My countrymen, enlightened sons of France:
    Ye—ye, who comprehend *true* freedom!
    Boldly trample on the groveling hearts
    Of those who still adhere to kings—and priests.
    Free as the air, and equal as its surface,
    Citizens! Patriots! Spill your bravest blood;
    Raise high the pile of slaughtered sycophants!
    Exterminate all those who dare presume
    To check this radiant dawn of liberty,
    Which soon shall blaze a full meridian sun
    too bright for despots and their cringing slaves
    To look on! Dazzled by its brilliancy,
    Unable to behold the great, resplendent,
    Full-orbited, mighty, glorious, liberty,
    Their narrow hearts will sink within their breasts
    Ignobly chained to proud nobility—
    To treacherous crowns—and wily priestcraft!
    Not daring to complain—much less redress
    The most oppressive burdens—meanly they
    Drag on existence in debasing bonds—
    In bonds which ye great, deserving Frenchmen
    Have so gloriously burst asunder.
    By yourselves ye are emancipated.

Live! Live to triumph in the enjoyment
Of reason and its rights. Never suffer
Those dear rights again to be invaded.
Let no ambitious, traitorous, haughty despot
Chain your minds or bodies more—but be free!
Frenchmen! Countrymen! My brethren! Be free.
Stain your swords with the purple tide flowing
From dying conspirators. Let the foes
Of our liberty bleed. They are vipers.
Let not bread which should nourish true Frenchmen
Be wasted on them! No! Destroy—destroy!
Justice calls aloud, destroy! Well ye know
Whose blood to spill—and whose to spare—without
The tedious mockeries of courts and judges.
Judge for yourselves—and quickly execute.

Francis the First

Fanny Kemble
1832

Scene: the court of Francis the First

Dramatic
Gonzales: a Spanish monk, 40–60, a man consumed with the need to avenge his sister's death

Gonzales has become a part of the French Court in order to ruin Laval, a nobleman whose father destroyed his sister.

GONZALES: In love with Bourbon! by this living light,
My mission here is well night bootless, then.
Now might I back to Spain, since Charles' objects
Are all defeated by this woman's passion,
Were there not yet another task, the dearest,
The labour that is life—mine own revenge!
Till I have reached that goal, my foot shall never
Tread its own soil; or, freed from its disguise—
This noiseless sandal of slow-gaited priesthood—
Resume its manly garb. Oh, very long
Is the accomplishment; but it is sure—
Sure as the night that curtains up each day—
Sure as that death which is the end of life.
Lie still, thou thirsty spirit, that within
Callst for the blood that *shall* allay thy craving!
Down, down with thee, until the hour be come
When I can fling this monkish treachery by,
Rush on my prey, and let my soul's hot flame
Lick up his blood, and quench it in his life!
Time, and the all-enduring soul that never
Shrinks from the trial, be my speed! and nought
My hope, my spur, my instrument, my end,
Save hate—eternal hate—immeasurable hate!

Ghosts

Ibsen, Trans. by Brian Johnston and Rick Davis
1881

Scene: the country estate in West Norway

Dramatic
Pastor Manders: a self-aggrandizing clergyman, 40—50

Here, the unctuous Manders confronts Helene Alving, the widow of his childhood friend who is soon to be honored with a memorial. The good pastor disapproves of Helene's parenting skills, and minces no words telling her so.

PASTOR MANDERS: All your life you've been ruled by a disastrously rebellious spirit. Your longings have drawn you toward everything undisciplined and lawless. You would never tolerate the slightest restraint. You've recklessly and irresponsibly tossed aside every inconvenience in your life, like some package you could just put down at will. It didn't please you to be a wife any longer, and so you left your husband. Being a mother was too much trouble, and so you turned your child loose with strangers. (…)
And in so doing, you've become a stranger to him. (…)
You *are*. You *must* be! And look at the state in which you got him back! Consider well, Mrs. Alving. You trespassed against your husband; this memorial you're raising to him shows you admit this in your heart. Now admit, as well, that you have trespassed against your son; there might still be time to turn him away from his errors. Turn away yourself—and save what can still be saved in him. For truly *(With raised forefinger.)* —truly, Mrs. Alving, you are a profoundly guilty woman. I've considered it my duty to tell you this.

The Great Galeoto

Jose Echegaray, Trans. by Hannah Lynch
1881

Scene: Madrid

Dramatic
Ernest: a passionate young man with poetic aspirations, 26

Ernest has been working on a drama for the stage. When asked by his patron to describe it, he laments the impossibility of creating a character who represents everyone.

ERNEST: Look! Each individual of this entire mass, each head of this monster of a thousand heads, of this Titan of the century, whom I call *everybody,* takes part in my play for a flying moment, utters but one word, flings a single glance. Perhaps his action consists of a smile. He appears but to vanish. Listless and absent-minded, he acts without passion, without anger, without guile, often for mere distraction's sake. (...)
These light words, these fugitive glances, these indifferent smiles, all these evanescent sounds and this trivial evil, which may be called the insignificant rays of the dramatic light, condensed to one focus, to one group, result in conflagration or explosion, in strife and in victims. If I represent the whole by a few types or symbolical personages, I bestow upon each one that which is really dispersed among many, and such a result distorts my idea. I must bring types on the stage whose guile repels and is the less natural because evil in them has no object. This exposes me to a worse consequence, to the accusation of meaning to paint a cruel, corrupted, and debased society, when my sole intention is to prove that not even the most insignificant actions are in themselves insignificant or lost for good or evil. For, concentrated by the mysterious influences of modern life, they may reach to immense effects.

The Importance of Being Earnest:
A Trivial Comedy for Serious People

Oscar Wilde

1895

Scene: London

Serio-Comic
Jack: a man with the wrong name, 20–30

*Here, the irascible Jack informs Lady Bracknell that he has
no intention of allowing his ward, Cecily, to marry her
nephew, Algernon.*

JACK: I beg your pardon for interrupting you, Lady Bracknell, but this
engagement is quite out of the question. I am Miss Cardew's
guardian, and she cannot marry without my consent until she
comes of age. That consent I absolutely decline to give. (…)
It pains me very much to speak frankly to you, Lady Bracknell,
about your nephew, but the fact is that I do not approve at all
of his moral character. I suspect him of being untruthful. (…)
I fear there can be no possible doubt about the matter. This
afternoon, during my temporary absence in London on an
important question of romance, he obtained admission to my
house by means of the false pretence of being my brother.
Under an assumed name he drank, I've just been informed by
my butler, an entire pint bottle of my Perrier-Jouet, Brut, '89; a
wine I was specially reserving for myself. Continuing his dis-
graceful deception, he succeeded in the course of the afternoon
in alienating the affections of my only ward. He subsequently
stayed to tea, and devoured every single muffin. And what
makes his conduct all the more heartless is, that he was perfect-
ly well aware from the first that I have no brother, that I never
had a brother, and that I don't intend to have a brother, not
even of any kind. I distinctly told him so myself yesterday afternoon.

John Gabriel Borkman

Ibsen, Trans. by Rolf Fjelde
1896

Scene: Norway

Dramatic
John Gabriel Borkman: a man led to ruination by ambition, 50s

John Gabriel Borkman sacrificed everything, including Ella, the woman he loved, to advance his banking career. Years later, he has lost everything. When Ella returns to confront him, John Gabriel sinks into despair. On a cold night the two visit a place where they used to sit and dream of a future that never was to be. Here, John Gabriel confesses that he never stopped loving Ella.

BORKMAN: *(More and more exhilarated.)* Oh, but all of this—it's only a kind of outworks enclosing the kingdom, you know! (…) My kingdom, of course! The kingdom I was on the verge of possessing when I—when I died. (…)
And now it lies there—defenseless, leaderless—exposed to the rape and plunder of thieves—! Ella! Do you see those mountain ranges *there*—far off. One after another. They leap skyward. They tower in space. That's my deep, my endless, inexhaustible kingdom! (…)
[The] wind works on me like the breath of life. It comes to me like a greeting from captive spirits. I can sense them, the buried millions. I feel the veins of metal, reaching their curving, branching, beckoning arms out to me. I saw them before me like living shadows—the night I stood in the bank vault with a lantern in my hand. You wanted your freedom then—and I tried to set you free. But I lacked the strength for it. Your treasures sank back in the depths. *(His hand outstretched.)* But I'll whisper to you here in the silence of the night. I love you, lying there unconscious in the depths and the darkness! I love you, you riches straining to be born—with all your shining aura of power and glory! I love you, love you, love you!

Manfred

Lord Byron
1817

Scene: a castle in the Alps

Dramatic
Manfred: a man tortured by his past, 20–30

*Manfred, a necromancer, is determined to summon the
ghost of the woman he loved to seek forgiveness for having
caused her death.*

MANFRED: We are the fools of time and terror: Days
 Steal on us and steal from us; yet we live,
 Loathing our life, and dreading still to die.
 In all the days of this detested yoke—
 This vital weight upon the struggling heart,
 Which sinks with sorrow, or beats quick with pain,
 Or joy that ends in agony or faintness—
 In all the days of past and future, for
 In life there is no present, we can number
 How few, how less than few, wherein the soul
 Forbears to pant for death, and yet draws back
 As from a stream in winter, though the chill
 Be but a moment's. I have one resource
 Still in my science—I can call the dead,
 And ask them what it is we dread to be:
 The sternest answer can but be the Grave,
 And that is nothing;—if they answer not—
 The buried Prophet answered to the Hag
 Of Endor; and the Spartan Monarch drew
 From the Byzantine maid's unsleeping spirit
 An answer and his destiny—he slew
 That which he loved, unknowing what he slew,
 And died unpardon'd—though he call'd in aid
 The Phyxian Jove, and in Phigalia roused
 The Arcadian Evocators to compel
 The indignant shadow to despose her wrath,

Or fix her term of vengeance—she replied
In words of dubious import, but fulfill'd.
If I had never lived, that which I love
Had still be living; had I never loved,
That which I love would still be beautiful—
Happy and giving happiness. What is she?
What is she now?—a sufferer for my sins—
A thing I dare not think upon—or nothing.
Within few hours I shall not call in vain—
Yet in this hour I dread the thing I dare:
Until this hour I never shrunk to gaze
On spirit, good or evil—now I tremble,
And feel a strange cold thaw upon my heart.
But I can act even what I most abhor,
And champion human fears.—The night approaches.

Manfred

Lord Byron
1817

Scene: a castle in the Alps

Dramatic
Manfred: a man tortured by his past, 20–30

When he has successfully summoned the spirit of Astarte, he begs her forgiveness.

MANFRED: Hear me, hear me—
    Astarte! my beloved! speak to me:
    I have so much endured, so much endure—
    Look on me! the grave hath not changed thee more
    Than I am changed for thee. Thou lovedst me
    Too much, as I loved thee: we were not made
    To torture thus each other, though it were
    The deadliest sin to love as we have loved.
    Say that thou loath'st me not, that I do bear
    This punishment for both, that thou wilt be
    One of the blessed, and that I shall die;
    For hitherto all hateful things conspire
    To bind me in existence—in a life
    Which makes me shrink from immortality—
    A future like the past. I cannot rest
    I know not what I ask, nor what I seek:
    I feel but what thou art—and what I am;
    And I would hear yet once before I perish
    The voice which was my music—Speak to me!
    For I have call'd on thee in the still night,
    Startled the slumbering birds from the hush'd boughs,
    And woke the mountain wolves, and made the caves
    Acquainted with thy vainly echo'd name,
    Which answer'd me—many things answer'd me—
    Spirits and men—but thou wert silent all.
    Yet speak to me! I have outwatch'd the stars,
    And gazed o'er heaven in vain in search of thee.

Speak to me! I have wander'd o'er the earth,
And never found thy likeness—Speak to me!
Look on the fiends around—they feel for me:
I fear them not, and feel for thee alone.
Speak to me! though it be in wrath;—but say—
I reck not what—but let me hear thee once—
This once—once more!

Masks and Faces

Charles Reade
1852

Scene: London

Serio-Comic
James Triplet: a starving artist, 30s

Here, the hapless Triplet pays a visit to Covet Garden only to find that his plays have been rejected and his children will have to go hungry.

TRIPLET: I knew it. I sent him three tragedies. They are accepted; and he has left me a note in the hall, to fix the reading—at last. I felt it must come, soon or late; and it has come—late. Master of three arts, painting, writing, and acting, by each of which men grow fat, how was it possible I should go on perpetually starving? But that is all over now. My tragedies will be acted, the town will have an intellectual treat, and my wife and children will stab my heart no more with their hungry looks. *(Call-boy enters with parcel.)*
Why, how is this? Oh, I see, he returns them for some trifling alterations. Well, if they are judicious, I shall certainly adopt them, for *(Opening the parcel.)* managers are practical men. My tragedies!—Eh? here are but two! one is accepted!—no! they are all here. *(Sighs.)* Well, *(Spitefully.)* it is a thousand pounds out of Mr. Rich's pocket! poor man! I pity him; and my hungry mouths at home! Heaven knows where I am to find bread for them tomorrow! Every thing that will raise a shilling I have sold or pawned. Even my poor picture here, the portrait of Mrs. Woffington from memory—I tried to sell that this morning at every dealer's in Long Acre—and not one would make me an offer.

The Night Before the Trial

Anton Chekhov, Trans. by Carol Rocamora
Circa 1890s

Scene: a gloomy way station, somewhere in provincial Russia

Tragicomedic
Aleksey Alekseich Zaytsev; a traveler, 30s

A young man, desperate, on the eve of his trial for bigamy, forgery, and attempted murder, contemplates suicide.

ZAYTSEV: *(removing his fur coat and felt boots).* God, it's freezing! My brain's gone numb, it's so cold…Feel as if I've been covered with snow, doused with water, and then flogged senseless…I mean, what with the snow drifts and the miserable blizzard, five minutes more out there and I'd be at death's door. I'm half-dead already. And for what? It'd be one thing if I were on my way to a "rendezvous", or to collect an inheritance or some-thing, but no, here I am, on the road to ruin…Can't even think about it, it's so terrible…Tomorrow there's a session of the cir-cuit court in town, and guess who's the defendant?! …They'll charge me with bigamy, forgery of my grandmother's will to the tune of three hundred rubles, roughly, and attempted murder of a billiards' marker. The jury'll throw me in prison—no doubt about it. Here today, emprisoned tomorrow, and in six month's time—it's the frozen wilds of Siberia…Brrrrrr! *(Pause.)* However, there is a way out of this terrible fix. Indeed, there is! If the jury finds me guilty, I shall turn to the aid of an old, old friend…A true and trusty friend! *(Pulls a large pistol from his suitcase.)* Ta-da! What a pal! Swapped him with Cheprakov for a couple of hounds. What a beauty! I mean, even to shoot yourself with him would bring you pleasure…of sorts …*(Gently.)* You loaded, fella? Eh? *(In a light voice, as if answering for the pistol.)* Yes, I am… *(In his own voice again.)* You'll make a lot of noise, won't you? A great big bang, right? *(In a light voice.)* A great big bang…*(In his own voice again.)* You clown, you…you old sweetheart…Go on, take a rest, go to sleep, "'night 'night" …*(Kisses the pistol and hides it in his suitcase.)* Soon as I hear "yes, guilty", then it's "bang! "—I'll put a bullet right through my brain, and that's that ...If only I weren't so frozen stiff... Brrrrr! Got to warm up...*(Waves his arms about, jumps up and down next to the stove.)* Brrrr!

On the Harmful Effects of Tabacco

Anton Chekhov, Trans. by Carol Rocamora
1886

Scene: the stage of an auditorium in a provincial Russian town

Tragicomedic
Ivan Ivanovich Nyukhin: husband of the proprietess of a boarding school for young ladies: 30s-40s

Tyrannized by his wife to give a public lecture on the harmful effects of smoking tobacco, a miserable, hen-pecked schoolteacher departs from his assigned topic to open his heart to the audience.

NYUKHIN: Oh, if only you knew how much I wanted to run away! *(Passionately.)* To run, to throw everything to the winds and just run, without once looking back… and where? It doesn't matter where …if only to run from this vulgar, rotten, worthless, good-for-nothing life, which has made an old man of me, a pitiful, pathetic old fool, a wretched old idiot, to run from this stupid, petty, shallow, miserable, miserable, miserable miser, to run from my wife, who has tortured me for thirty-three years, to run from the conservatory, the kitchen, from my wife's money, from all this stupidity and vulgarity…and stop somewhere far far away, out in a field somewhere, and stand there like a tree, or a telegraph pole, or a scarecrow, under the wide-open sky, and gaze all night at the silent moon shining above, and forget, forget…Oh, how I wish never again to remember, never!…How I long to tear off this wretched old coat, the coat in which I was married thirty years ago…(tears off coat) the coat in which I give my never-ending lectures for charitable purposes…Take that! (Throws coat on ground and tramples on it.) And that! I'm old, and poor, and pathetic, like this shabby old waistcoat with its threadbare seams… *(Indicates the back.)* I don't want anything! I'm above all this! Once upon a time I was young, and brilliant, I went to the university, I had dreams, I was a human being…And now, now I want nothing! Nothing, only leave me in peace…leave me in peace! *(Glances around, puts on his coat.)* There's my wife, she's waiting out there in the wings…She's come at last, and she's waiting for me…*(Looks at his watch.)* We're out of time…If she asks you, then please, I beg of you, tell her that the lecture did take place…and that the dummy—that is to say, me, that I conducted myself with complete decorum. *(Looks around, clears his throat.)* She's looking this way…*(Raises his voice.)* "And thus, in conclusion, based on the evidence presented here today, as I have proven, that tobacco is a terribly poisonous substance, it therefore follows that you should not smoke under any circumstances, and I venture to say, furthermore, that I hope that my lecture 'on the harmful effects of tobacco' has been of benefit to you, to whatever extent." There. I've said it. And now I feel much better. (…) *(Bows and exits majestically.)*

On the High Road

Anton Chekhov, Trans. by Carol Rocamora
1885

Scene: a tavern somewhere in southern Russia

Dramatic
Semeon Sergeevich Bortsov: a ruined landowner, 40s–50s

*His property lost, desperate and destitute, Bortsov implores
a tavernkeeper for a drink.*

BORTSOV: *(Goes up to the bar.)* Hit me again! For Christ's sake! (…)
Just one little glass…that's all. Come on…put it on my tab! I'll
pay you! (…)
Please! I beg of you! (…)
You don't understand me! Listen, you boor, get it into that
thick peasant head of yours, if you have an ounce of brains,
that is, it's not me that's asking for it, it's my insides, to put it in
language that you can understand, you peasant, it's my guts
that are asking for it! It's my sickness that's asking for it!
Understand? (…)
Look, if I don't get a drink right now, see, if I don't satisfy this
raging thirst, I'm going to do something terrible. God only
knows what I might do! You've seen lots of drunks in your
time, I imagine, you low-life, don't tell me you don't know what
they're like by now! They're sick! Chain 'em up, beat 'em up,
knife 'em, even, as long as you give 'em their vodka! I humbly
beg of you! I beseech you! I'm groveling! My God, how I'm
groveling! (…)
Where am I going to get money, anyway? I've spent it all on
drink! All of it! So what am I going to give you? All I've got
left is my overcoat, and I can't give you that…I don't have any
clothes on underneath! How about a hat? *(Takes off his hat
and offers it.)* (…)
Don't want that? In that case, put it on my tab. Soon as I get
back from town, I'll bring you your five kopek piece! I hope
you choke on it! Do you hear me? Choke on it! I hope it
sticks in your throat! *(Coughs.)* I hate you!

On the High Road

Anton Chekhov, Trans. by Carol Rocamora
1885

Scene: a tavern somewhere in southern Russia

Dramatic
Yegor Merik: a tramp, any age

*Merik describes demons and other apparitions to the super-
stitious patrons of a tavern in the remote parts of southern
Russia.*

MERIK: *(makes a bed for himself on a bench).* Well, it's obvious,
you've never seen a devil, if you think *I'm* one. That's not what
a devil looks like. (Lies down and places his hatchet along side
of him.) Go to sleep, little hachet, my sweet little friend…I'll
cover up your handle for you (…)
Where did I get this hachet? Stole it…Stole it, and now I carry
it everywhere with me, I'm stuck with it…sort of…pity to throw
it away…don't know what else to do with it. It's like a wife
you're sick of…Yes… *(Covers it up.)* No, devils aren't like me,
my friend… (…)
They're like spirit… or air… Go on—breathe *(he exhales)*…
they're like that. You can't even see 'em. (…)
No…devils, demons, ghosts, you can't see any of 'em…The eye
wasn't made to see everything . . . When I was little, I'd sneak
out into the woods at night, to see all the wood demons… I'd
call and I'd call for the spirits to come out, I wouldn't dare blink
an eye, even…saw all kinds of creatures, but never saw a wood
demon. Went to the graveyard at night in the churchyard,
looking for ghosts—but that was old wives' tales, too. Saw all
kinds of animals, but as for a spirit, you know, one who could
frighten you—forget about it. The eye just can't see 'em…

Peer Gynt

Ibsen, Trans. by Rolf Fjelde
1867

Scene: an onion field

Serio-Comic
Peer Gynt: a man in search of himself, 30s

Following many misadventures, the foolish Peer Gynt finally achieves a moment of insight as he begins to peel an onion.

PEER: *(Calling after them.)* Thank you, boys and girls—and all you good people—for your kindness to me. *(He sits weakly down on the headstone, stares dully around him and leans heavily and forlornly on his stick.)* Religion and playing the fool may be all right, but a man's belly is the real voice. *(He scratches along the earth with his stick, finds something that interests him. He bends down and pulls it up.)* An onion. *(Chuckling.)* John the Baptist, they say, ate locusts and wild honey. I'm reduced to an onion. But then he was nothing but a preacher—and I—I'm an emperor. *(Shaking his head.)* You old fool prophet, you're no emperor, you're a—an onion. *(He sneezes, his eyes watering.)* And yes sir, old Peer Gynt, I'm going to peel you layer by layer. *(He plucks a layer off the onion and chews it.)* Tastes like Peer Gynt all right. *(He spits it out and goes on peeling.)* Ahah. Here's the fellow that dug for gold. Hmn. There's no juice in him if he ever had any. And here's a piece of rough hide with a hard edge. That must be when I was a fur trapper up there at Hudson's Bay. I was devilish tough then. *(Peering down at the onion.)* Here's something shaped like a crown—no thank you. *(He shudders and grimaces in sour remembrance.)* And here's the archeologist and here the prophet. *(He puts his finger to his nose.)* He stinks. He brings water to the eyes of an honest man. Here are two layers all rolled lovingly together. This is Peer Gynt living in pleasure and sin. And here is one with black streaks in it. Either the black cloth of a preacher or the skin of a Negro. *(He plucks several layers at the same time.)* What is an onion anyhow? Layer after layer. Where is the core, where is it—the onion's self? *(He breaks the rest of the onion apart.)* Damned if he's got any self. Right down to the center he's nothing but layers—smaller and smaller. *(Cynically.)* Nature is a joke.

The Philanderer

George Bernard Shaw
1898

Scene: London

Serio-Comic
Paramore: a self-styled medical researcher, 40s

*While reading through the British Medical Journal,
Paramore discovers that the disease he believes himself to
have discovered cannot exist. Here, the ridiculous "scientist"
vows to prove the disease really does exist.*

PARAMORE: *(Despairingly.)* The worst of news! Terrible news! Fatal news! My disease— (…)
(Fiercely.) [I mean my disease:] Paramore's disease: the disease I discovered: the work of my life! Look here! *(He points to the journal with a ghastly expression of horror.)* If this is true, it was all a mistake: there is no such disease. (…)
(Hoarsely.) It's natural for you to think only of yourself. I don't blame you: all invalids are selfish. Only a scientific man can feel what I feel now. *(Writhing under a sense of intolerable injustice.)* It's the fault of the wickedly sentimental laws of this country. I was not able to make experiments enough: only three dogs and a monkey. Think of that, with all Europe full of my professional rivals! men burning to prove me wrong! There is freedom in France: enlightened republican France! One Frenchman experiments on two hundred monkeys to disprove my theory. Another sacrifices £36—three hundred dogs at three francs apiece—to upset the monkey experiments. A third proves them both wrong by a single experiment in which he gets the temperature of a camel's liver sixty degrees below zero. And now comes this cursed Italian who has ruined me. He has a government grant to buy animals with, besides having the run of the largest hospital in Italy. *(With desperate resolution.)* But I won't be beaten by any Italian. I'll go to Italy myself. I'll rediscover my disease: I know it exists; I feel it; and I'll prove it if I have to experiment on every mortal animal thats got a liver at all. *(He folds his arms and breathes hard at them.)*

Pillars of Society

Ibsen, Trans. by Rolf Fjelde
1877

Scene: a small Norwegian seaport

Dramatic
Bernick: a man being confronted by the woman he once rejected

Years ago, when Bernick chose another woman for his bride, heartbroken Lona made her way to America where she made a home in the wilderness. Years later, Lona has returned only to find the man she once loved changed into a duplicitous businessman who cares for nothing save his place in society. Here, Bernick complains bitterly of his position to Lona.

BERNICK: Lona, you must despise me. (…)
You have no right to, either. Not to *despise* me! Lona, you can't image how inexpressibly lonely I am here, in this small-minded, stunted community—how with every year I've had to pare down a few more of my hopes for a truly fulfilling existence. What have I accomplished, despite all it seems? Piecework— penny favors. But anything different, anything more wouldn't be tolerated here. If I wanted to move one step ahead of the sentiments and views cried up in the streets this morning, that would be the end of my power. You know what we are—we who've been labeled pillars of society. We're the puppets of society, no more than that.

Presumption; or,
The Fate of Frankenstein
Richard Brinksley Peake
1823

Scene: Geneva

Dramatic
Frankenstein: a man obsessed with discovering the secret of creation, 30s

Since beginning his quest, Frankenstein has been able to think of nothing else. Here, the scientist reflects on the nature of death before returning to his work.

FRANKENSTEIN: Every moment lost, fevers me. What time have I devoted? *(Rises.)* Had I not been heated by an almost supernatural enthusiasm, my application to this study would have been irksome, disgusting, and almost intolerable. To examine the causes of life—I have had recourse to death—I have seen how the fine form of man has been wasted and degraded—have beheld the corruption of death succeed to the blooming cheek of life! I have seen how the worm inherits the wonders of the eye and brain—I paused—analysing all the minutiae of causation as exemplified in the change of life from death—until from the midst of this darkness the sudden light broke in upon me! A light so brilliant and dazzling, some miracle must have produced the flash! The vital principle! The cause of life!—Like Prometheus of old, have I daringly attempted the formation— the animation of a Being! To my task—away with reflection—to my task—"to my task!"

Presumption; or,
The Fate of Frankenstein

Richard Brinksley Peake

1823

Scene: Geneva

Dramatic
Frankenstein: a man obsessed with discovering the secret of creation, 30s

When he successfully reanimates his monster, Frankenstein finally realizes that he has forfeited his soul.

FRANKENSTEIN: It lives! [It lives.] I saw the dull yellow eye of the creature open, it breathed hard, and a convulsive motion agitated its limbs. What a wretch have I formed, [his legs are in proportion and] I had selected his features as beautiful—"beautiful!" Ah, horror! his cadaverous skin scarcely covers the work of muscles and arteries beneath, his hair lustrous, black, and flowing—his teeth of pearly whiteness—but these luxuriances only form more horrible contrasts with the deformities of the Demon. *(Music. He listens at the foot of the staircase.)* [It is yet quiet—] What have I accomplished? the beauty of my dream has vanished! and breathless horror and disgust fill my heart. For this I have deprived myself of rest and health, "have worked my brain to madness;" and when I looked to reap my great reward, a flash breaks in upon my darkened soul, and tells me my attempt was impious, and that its fruition will be fatal to my peace for ever. *(He listens again.)* All is still! The dreadful spectre of a human form—no mortal could withstand the horror of that countenance [—a mummy endued with animation could be so hideous as [the wretch I have endowed with life!]—miserable and impious being that I am! [—lost—lost] Elizabeth! brother! Agatha!—faithful Agatha! never more dare I look upon your virtuous faces. "Lost! lost! lost!"

The Proposal

Anton Chekhov, Trans. by Carol Rocamora
1888

Scene: the drawing room of a country estate, somewhere in provincial Russia

Comedic
Ivan Vasilevich Lomov, a portly hypochondriac, 40–50s

Lomov, a neurotic, hypochondriacal landowner, summons up his courage and calls on a neighbor to propose marriage to his daughter.

LOMOV: *(alone)* God, it's cold… I'm shivering all over, like a schoolboy before an exam. Act now! …that's the main thing. He who hesitates is lost: wait around for true love, for ideal love, and you'll never get married…Brrrrr!…It's cold…Natalya Stepanovna is an excellent housekeeper, she's not bad-looking, she's educated…what more could I want? Only now I'm so agitated I've got ringing in my ears. *(Takes a drink of water.)* Anyway, I can't *not* get married…I mean, first of all, I'm already thirty-five years old—I'm at that critical age, so to speak. Second of all, I've got to settle down, lead an orderly life…I've got heart trouble, constant palpitations, I get agitated easily, I'm always worked up about something or other…Look, right now, how my lips are trembling and my right eyelid is twitching…But the worst thing is, trying to get some sleep. No sooner do I get in bed and fall asleep, when all of a sudden—whoosh!—I get this pain in my left side, and it goes right to my shoulder and then to my head…I leap up, like some sort of madman, I walk around for a bit, and then I lie down again, but no sooner do I fall asleep, when suddenly—whoosh!—there it is again! I mean, if it happens once, it happens twenty times…

Rosmersholm

Ibsen, Trans. by Rolf Fjelde
1886

Scene: Rosmersholm, an old manor house in West Norway

Serio-Comic
Ulrik Brendel: a teacher, down on his luck, 50–60

*When Brendel arrives unannounced at the home of his for-
mer student, John Rosmer, everyone is surprised by his
shabby appearance. When a young woman of the household remarks that she has read many of his books, the professor claims that his best thoughts have never been put on
paper.*

BRENDEL: You recall, *mein Johannes,* that I'm something of a sybarite.
Ein Feinschmecker. And have been, all my days. I love to savor
things in solitude. Because then my pleasure doubles, yes, ten
times over. So you see—whenever golden dreams poured over
me and engulfed me—whenever new ideas unfolded, dazzlingly
and boundlessly within me, lifting me to the heights on their
soaring wings—then I formed them into poems, visions, images.
I mean, into their equivalents, you understand. (…)
The ecstasies I've relished in my time, John! The mysterious
beatitude of creation—or, again, its equivalent—the plaudits,
the acclaim, the celebrity, the laurel crowns—all these I've gath-
ered in my grateful hands, trembling with joy. In most secret
imaginings, I've known such exaltation—that my mind goes
reeling into space.

Salome
Oscar Wilde
1894

Scene: the court of Herod

Dramatic
Jokanaan: John the Baptist, 30s

When Jokanaan is released from Cistern so that Salome may see him, he calls out for Herod and Herodias.

JOKANAAN: Where is he whose cup of abominations is now full? Where is he, who in a robe of silver shall one day die in the face of all the people? Bid him come forth, that he may hear the voice of him who hath cried in the waste places and in the houses of kings. (…)
Where is she who saw the images of men painted on the walls, even the images of the Chaldeans painted with colours, and gave herself up unto the lust of her eyes, and sent ambassadors into the land of Chaldea? (…)
Where is she who gave herself unto the Captains of Assyria, who have baldricks on their loins, and crowns of many colours on their heads? Where is she who hath given herself to the young men of the Egyptians, who are clothed in fine linen and hyacinth, whose shields are of gold, whose helmets are of silver, whose bodies are mighty? Go bid her rise up from the bed of her abominations, from the be of her incestuousness, that she may hear the words of him who prepareth the way of the Lord, that she may repent her of her iniquities. Though she will not repent, but will stick fast in her abominations; go, bid her come, for the fan of the Lord is in His hand.

Smiles and Tears; or,
The Widow's Stratagem

Marie-Therese DeCamp
1815

Scene: London

Serio-Comic
Colonel O'Donolan: a jealous hot-head, 20–30

O'Donolan is in love with the capricious Lady Emily, who does her best to keep the poor man guessing. When she claims ignorance of his suffering, O'Donolan turns to an older woman for support.

O'DONOLAN: Why will I? O! and is it myself that wishes it? now here's Mrs. Belmore, who knows what a fool I am, and how distractedly I am devoted to you—she shall judge between us—Lady Emily asks why I am upon the rack; can I be otherwise, when a whole week will sometimes elapse, without my being able to obtain so much as a work or a look—I have been at her door every hour in the day—I have not gone away from it, before I have come back again; and yet, I have not been able to catch a glimpse of her—my only chance of seeing her now, is in public places, or assemblies, where the devil a bit can I see her at all; for she is so everlastingly surrounded by a herd of coxcombs, pouring flattery into her ears, that 'tis impossible to get near her. (…)

Ah, now! and did I ever expect it? No, upon my honour!—But a look,—if you would only give me a look, just to say, O, you're there, are you! I should be satisfied: but no such luck for *me!*—it's a nod to one, a shake of the hand with another, a whisper to a third! and while I am kicking my heels in a corner, I have the mortification of seeing her led off in triumph to her carriage by some stupid fellow, who would be deemed too great an ass to stand behind it—then do I return home to pass a sleepless night, and dream of the miseries I've endured through the day.

Swan Song

Anton Chekhov, Trans. by Carol Rocamora.
1887

Scene: the empty stage of a provincial theatre, late at night,
following a performance

Tragicomedic
Vasily Vasilich Svetlovidov, an old character actor, 68

*Stumbling out drunk onto an empty stage in a dark, desert-
ed theatre, an old character has-been actor faces the empty
dreams of his career.*

SVETLOVIDOV: Well, well, well, what do you know? What-do-you-
know! That's a fine kettle of fish! That's a fine how-do-you- do!
Fell asleep in the dressing room, didn't I? Show's over, theatre's
empty, everyone's gone home, and I'm left behind, snoring
away, like an old saw. You old relic, you! You old fossil! Had
one too many, dropped off without knowing it, didn't you? You
old mummy! *(Calls out.)* Yegorka! Yegorka, you devil! Damn
you! Petrushka! Out cold, the devils...curse 'em! Yegorka!
(Takes a stool, sits on it and places the candle on the floor.)
Silence...Only an echo...that's all...Yegorka and
Petrushka...three rubles apiece they got from me today...for
their 'diligence'...won't find them around here any more, thank
you very much...gone, probably locked the theatre up behind
them, too, the miserable wretches...*(Shakes his head.)* Drunk!
Ach! A benefit performance, thank you very much, and all that
wine and beer they poured down my throat tonight...good
God! My body's a sponge, I've got twelve tongues rolling
around in my mouth...Disgusting! (Pause.) Stupid, isn't it...The
old fool—drunk again, and in the name of what...Ach! Good
God! My back aches, my head aches, I feel feverish all over...
but in my soul, it's cold...and dark...like a cave. All right, so
ruin your health, who cares, but at least take pity on your old
age, Vasilich, you fool...
(Pause.) Old age...Go on, play your games, put on the mask,
play the fool...your life's over...sixty-eight years old and you've

had it, yes, you have! Too late!...You've drained the bottle...
there's nothing left...only the dregs...So...Too bad, Vasyusha...
that's the way it goes ...Like it or not, time to rehearse the part
of the corpse...Old mother death waiting for her cue...*(Looks
around)* ...Do you know, I've been on the stage for forty-five
years now, and it's the first time I've seen an empty theatre at
night...Yes, the very first time ...Funny, isn't it...Curse it...*(Goes
to the footlights.)* Can't see a goddamn thing...Wait...prompter
box... music stand ...stalls ...and beyond? Darkness! A black
hole, a yawning grave, where death herself is lurking!...
Brrrrr!...cold! A draft from the hall, cold, like an empty chim-
ney, ghosts drifting down the aisles...sends chills up your spine!
(Calls out). Yegorka! Petrushka! Where are you, damn it? Good
God, why do I curse much! Stop it! Stop this swearing! Stop
this drinking—you're too old... time to die...At sixty-eight,
respectable people, they get up, they go to church, they prepare themselves for death, and you...Good God! Just look at
you! Profanity! Debauchery! Buffoonery!
...You're not fit to be seen! Got to get dressed...Terrifying!
Could have sat here all night...could have died of fright...*(Goes
toward his dressing room.)*

Two Roses

James Albery
1870

Scene: London

Serio-Comic
Wyatt: a disgruntled suitor, 20s

Wyatt, a pragmatic country lad here offers astute commentary on his fashionable London counterparts.

WYATT: I feel grateful when I see a nobly dressed swell. There's a fine thoughtfulness of others about him; such fellows as you and I spend our money on books and beer, and pamper our wits and our wallets for our own special enjoyment. But a swell he gets himself up for others, and he makes himself fine for me to look at. He pays himself for buttons and rings and chains for me to admire. He charges me nothing to see him; I don't have to get a ticket, but he comes out and I have a front place gratis. He don't even want me to applaud, but goes on perseveringly in spite of the debts and pains, making himself beautiful to see, and perhaps while I'm enjoying his patent boots, he's suffering from corns. Oh, he's a noble creature is a swell.

Uncle Tom's Cabin

George L. Aiken
1852

Scene: New Orleans

Dramatic
St. Clare: a gentleman, 30–40

*When St. Clare's northern cousin objects to his young
daughter's lavishing much affection on his new slave, Uncle
Tom, he gives his relative a lecture on northern hypocrisy.*

ST. CLARE: You would think no hard in a child's caressing a large dog
even if he was black; but a creature that can think, reason and
feel, and is immortal, you shudder at. Confess it, cousin. I know
the feeling among some of you Northerners well enough. Not
that there is a particle of virtue in our not having it, but custom
with us does what Christianity ought to do: obliterates the feeling of personal prejudice. You loathe them as you would a
snake or a toad, yet you are indignant at their wrongs. You
would not have them abused but you don't want to have anything to do with them yourselves. Isn't that it? (…)
What would the poor and lowly do without children? Your little
child is your only true democrat. Tom, now, is a hero to Eva; his
stories are wonders in her eyes; his songs and Methodist hymns
are better than an opera, and the traps and little bits of trash in
his pockets a mine of jewels, and he the most wonderful Tom
that ever wore a black skin. This is one of the roses of Eden that
the Lord has dropped down expressly for the poor and lowly,
who get few enough of any other kind.

When We Dead Awaken

Ibsen, Trans. by Rolf Fjelde
1899

Scene: a health resort by the sea

Serio-Comic
Professor Arnold Rubek: a sculptor, 40s

As Rubek and his wife, Maja, enjoy a quiet moment at a spa, their conversation turns to his work. Here, the world-weary artist reveals the dark secrets to be found in the simple portrait busts he sculpts for wealthy patrons.

RUBEK: *(With a sly smile.)* It's not simply portrait busts that I model, Maja. (…)
[But] they're not portrait busts, pure and simple; that's what I'm saying. (…)
There's something hidden, something sinister behind and within those busts—a secret something that ordinary people can't see— (…)
(His tone arbitrary.) Only I can see it. And it amuses me no end. On the surface is that so-called "striking likeness" that everyone stands and gapes at, transfixed. *(His voice dropping.)* But down at the deepest core are respectable and worthy horse faces and the stubborn muzzles of mules—lop-eared, low-browed dog skulls, and pampered pig snouts—and every so often, the heavy, brutal semblance of a bull— (…)
Only the dear, domestic animals, Maja. All the animals that human beings have distorted in their own image. And that have distorted human beings in return. *(Drains his champagne glass and laughs.)* And these perfidious works of art are what the virtuous rich come and order from me. And pay for in good faith—and through the nose, too. They're almost worth their weight in gold, to coin a phrase.

Widowers Houses

George Bernard Shaw
1898

Scene: England

Dramatic
Sartorius: a wealthy landlord, 50s

When his daughter's idealistic young suitor questions the living conditions in the slums he owns, the pragmatic Sartorius offers insight into his tenants' sociological tendencies.

SARTORIUS: *(Pitying his innocence.)* My young friend: these poor people do not know how to live in proper dwellings: they would wreck them in a week. You doubt me: try it for yourself. You are welcome to replace all the missing banisters, handrails, cistern lids and dusthole tops at your own expense; and you will find them missing again in less than three days: burnt, sir, every stick of them. I do not blame the poor creatures: they need fires, and often have no other way of getting them. But I really cannot spend pound after pound in repairs for them to pull down, when I can barely get them to pay me four and sixpence a week for a room, which is the recognized fair London rent. No, gentlemen: when people are very poor, you cannot help them, no matter how much you may sympathize with them. It does them more harm than good in the long run. I prefer to save my money in order to provide additional houses for the homeless, and to lay by a little for Blanche. *(He looks at them. They are silent: Trench unconvinced, but talked down; Cokane humanely perplexed. Sartorius bends his brows; comes forward in his chair as if gathering himself for a spring; and addresses himself, with impressive significance, to Trench.)* And now, Dr. Trench, may I ask what your income is derived from?

The Bonds of Interest

Jacinto Benavente, Trans. by John Garrett Underhill
1907

Scene: a garden in an imaginary country

Dramatic
Leander: a young man in love, 20–30

Leander has plotted with the unscrupulous Crispin to pretend to fall in love with the wealthy young Sylvia to gain her fortune. When Leander finds that he has truly fallen in love, he agonizes over his feelings.

LEANDER: I never believed it possible a man could love like this. I never believed that I could ever love. Through all my wandering life along the dusty roads, I was not only the one who passed, I was the one who fled, the enemy of the harvest and the field, the enemy of man, enemy of sunshine and the day. Sometimes the fruit of the wayside tree, stolen, not given, left some savor of joy on my parched lips, and sometimes, after many a bitter day, resting at night beneath the stars, the calm repose of heaven would invite and soothe me to a dream of something that might be in my life like that calm night sky, brooding infinite over my soul—serene! And so tonight, in the enchantment of this fête, it seemed to me as if there had come a calm, a peace into my life—and I was dreaming! Ah! How I did dream! But tomorrow it will be again the bitter flight with justice at our heels, and I cannot bear that they should take me here where she is, and where she may ever have cause to be ashamed at having known me.

The Gambler

Klabund

1920

Scene: Europe, 1920s

Dramatic
The Gambler: a man who has lost everything, 40–50

Here, a man addicted to the thrill of the wager describes his
experiences with Lady Luck.

THE GAMBLER: I've lost…I've lost it all…I'm finished…before I had even
begun…I had four queens in my hand…Four queens all at
once…ha, I thought, at last Fortune is smiling to the fourth
power…I bet ten thousand…my opponent was a skeleton
dressed in the latest fashion…a monstrous pumpkin-sized
skull…no hair, no flesh…No eyes, the five cards of a poker-hand
held motionless in his bony fingers…The skeleton squeaked out
twenty-thousand like a badly oiled velocipede. The man, I
thought, if he actually is a man, is crazy, totally idiotic…I've got
four queens in my hand, and he wants to up the ante, I shout
40,000 and my head range, throbbed with this verse:
> When Lady Luck comes as a fourfold treat,
> A man roams the fields, a fog in his head.
> What cares he for women in home or in street
> Or the narcissus wind when the twilight turns red?
80,000 cackled the skeleton…That's called making the best of
one's cards to the very last…You are life and he is death…You
have the world to win from him…Ah, immeasurable luck, if you
win eternal bliss…immortality. 160,000 I roared… 320,000
echoed the rattling anatomy…I computed feverishly… 160 and
80 and 40 and 20 and 10…total 310 thousand…all my faculties
were in play and at stake…What could I bet against his
320,000? Behind my chair stood Evelina…fair and delicate and
sweet as ever…she had gone pale…I turned around…I lifted my
arm onto the gaming-table…She closed her eyes and stood still
as a statuette…then I tore the silken dress from her body…and
her shift…She stood naked on the table…And I cry: Against

your 320,000 I bet my wife and my girl, my beloved and my goddess...Agreed? The skeleton grinned and ran his empty eye-holes over the blooming flesh of the young female body...Agreed, it bleated its assent, Evelina stood there leaning to one side...We tossed our cards on the table...he had four aces...I saw him wrap his black cape around Evelina...and lift her from the table...I heard his tinny voice order a car from a club waiter...I stumbled out into the black night...My fate is sealed.

The Game of Chess

Kenneth Sawyer Goodman

1914

Scene: a landowner's house in Russia

Dramatic
Boris: a young revolutionary, 20s

*Boris has entered the house of Alexis Alexandrovitch with
the intention of assassinating him. When the cruel
landowner reveals his knowledge of Boris's plot, the young
man explains his intentions.*

BORIS: I am a peasant. My father and my father's father were peasants. You are a noble. Your line runs back to Tartar princes. It is
a matter of centuries of pain and slavery against centuries of
oppression and violence. I take no account of today, only of yesterday and tomorrow. Your acts have been cruel and harsh,
doubtless, I hardly know. I throw them out of the scale. I throw
out my own sufferings. They are not enough in themselves to
tip the balance. You and I are nothing. It is caste against caste. I
gave myself to the revolutionary party, yes! I am their agent as
you say, but I know little of their ideas for Russia. I care less. I
only know that the band to which I belong represents the struggle which I feel in my own breast. I am their willing tool. I do
their will because the right of vengeance comes down to me in
the blood. (…)
It is my order against yours.

The Game of Chess

Kenneth Sawyer Goodman
1914

Scene: a landowner's house in Russia

Dramatic
Alexis Alexandrovitch: a despotic landowner, 40s

When he is confronted in his home by a would-be assassin, Alexandrovitch dismisses the young revolutionary's attempt with scorn.

ALEXIS: Ah, your order against mine, eh? Centuries of pain against centuries of oppression. Well, well! You set aside today, do you? You throw your own little pains and penalties out of the scale on one side, and my little tyrannies and floggings and acts of villainy out on the other? You see yourself only as the avenger of a caste against a caste. The right of vengeance and the need of it comes down to you in the blood, does it? You're exalted by the breath of dead peasants, are you? It's because of that and only because of it that you take pride in the work you've set your hand to. Huh! Grotesque! You strike the air with a rod of smoke. You've stumbled upon the essence of the inane. You're about to commit a fantastic mockery of Justice.

The Hairy Ape

Eugene O'Neill
1922

Scene: a transatlantic ocean liner

Dramatic
Yank: a stoker, 20–30

Here, crude Yank rallies his fellow shipmates.

YANK: *(Standing up and glaring at Long.)* Sit down before I knock
yuh down! *(Contemptuously.)* De Bible, huh? De Cap'tlist class,
huh? Aw nix on dat Salvation Army-Socialist bull. Git a soap-
box! Hire a hall! Come and be saved, huh? Jerk us to Jesus,
huh? Aw g'wan! I've listened to lots of guys like you, see.
Yuh're all wrong. Wanter know what I t'ink? Yuh ain't no good
for no one. Yuh're de bunk. Yuh ain't got no noive, get me?
Yuh're yellow, dat's what. Yellow, dat's you. Say! What's dem
slobs in de foist cabin got to do wit us? We're better men dan
dey are, ain't we? Sure! One of us guys could clean up de
whole mob wit one mit. Put one of 'em down here for one
watch in de stokehole, what'd happen? Dey'd carry him off on
a stretcher. Dem boids don't amount to nothin'. Dey're just baggage. Who makes dis old tub run? Ain't it us guys? Well den,
we belong, don't we? We belong and dey don't. Dat's all. As
for dis bein' hell—aw, nuts! Yuh lost your noive, dat's what. Dis
is a man's job, get me? It belongs. It runs dis tub. No stiffs need
apply. But yuh're a stiff, see? Yuh're yellow, dat's you.

The Hairy Ape

Eugene O'Neill
1922

Scene: a transatlantic ocean liner

Dramatic
Yank: a stoker, 20–30

When Yank frightens a young female passenger who was exploring the ships nether regions, he becomes furious at the invective she hurled his way at the height of her scare.

YANK: I scared her? Why de hell should I scare her? Who de hell is she? Ain't she de same as me? Hairy ape, huh? *(With his old confident bravado.)* I'll show her I'm better'n her, if she on'y knew it. I belong and she don't, see! I move and she's dead! Twenty-five knots a hour, dat's me! Dat carries her but I make dat. She's on'y baggage. Sure! *(Again bewilderedly.)* But, Christ, she was funny lookin'! Did yuh pipe her hands? White and skinny. Yuh could see de bones through 'em. And her mush, dat was dead white, too. And her eyes, dey was like dey'd seen a ghost. Me, dat was! Sure! Hairy ape! Ghost, huh? Look at dat arm! *(He extends his right arm, swelling out of the great muscles.)* I coulda took her wit dat, wit just my little finger even, and broke her in two. *(Again bewilderedly.)* Say, who is dat skoit, huh? What is she? What's she come from? Who made her? Who give her de noive to look at me like dat? Dis ting's got my goat right. I don't get her. She's new to me. What does a skoit like her mean, huh? She don't belong, get me! I can't see her. *(With growing anger.)* But one ting I'm wise to, aw right, aw right! Youse all kin bet your shoits I'll git even wit her. I'll show her if she tinks she—She grinds de organ and I'm on de string, huh? I'll fix her! Let her come down again and I'll fling her in de furnace! She'll move den! She won't shiver at nothin', den! Speed, dat'll be her! She'll belong den! *(He grins horribly.)*

The Lower Depths

Maxim Gorky, Trans. by Alexander Bakshy
1902

Scene: a crude flophouse in Russia

Dramatic
Satin: a thief, 40–50

*One of several miserable denizens of the flophouse, Satin
here shares a piece of alcohol-induced philosophy.*

SATIN: I'm in a kind mood today—the devil knows why. (…)
When I'm drunk I like everything. Yes, sir. He's praying? Fine. A
man can believe or not believe—it's his own affair. A man is
free—he pays for everything himself—for belief and disbelief,
for love, for intelligence, and that makes him free. Man—that's
the truth. What is man? It's not you, nor I, nor they—No, it's
you, I, they, the old man, Napoleon, Mohammed—all in one.
(Outlines the figure of a man in the air.) You understand? It's
tremendous! In this are all the beginnings and all the ends.
Everything in man, everything for man. Only man exists, the rest
is the work of his hands and his brain. Man! It's magnificent! It
has a proud ring! Man! We have to respect man, not pity him,
not demean him—Respect him, that's what we have to do. Let's
drink to man, Baron! *(Rises.)* It's good to feel oneself a man! I'm
a jailbird, a murderer, a cheat—granted! When I walk down the
street, people look at me as at a crook—they side-step and
glance back at me—and often say to me: Scoundrel! Charlatan!
Work! Work? For what? So that I have what my body needs
and feel satisfied? *(Laughs.)* I've always despised people whose
main thought in life is to feel satisfied. That's not important,
Baron—no! Man is above that! Man is above satisfaction!

The Man Who Married a Dumb Wife

Anatole France

1915

Scene: Paris

Serio-Comic
Leonard: a young judge, 30s

*Leonard has recently married a woman who cannot speak.
Here, he laments his choice.*

LEONARD: What! what! Don't you know, Master Adam, that I *have*
just been married? Yes, only last month, to a girl from one of
our best country families, young and handsome, Catherine
Momichel, the seventh daughter of the Criminal Court Judge at
Salency. But alas! she is dumb. Now you know my affliction.
(…)
Oh, I couldn't help noticing it, of course, but it didn't seem to
make so much difference to me then as it does now. I considered her beauty, and her property, and thought of nothing but
the advantages of the match and the happiness I should have
with her. But now these matters seem less important, and I do
wish she could talk; that would be a real intellectual pleasure
for me, and, what's more, a practical advantage for the household. What does a Judge need most in his house? Why, a good-
looking wife, to receive the suitors pleasantly, and, by subtle
suggestions, gently bring them to the point of making proper
presents, so that their cases may receive—more careful attention. People need to be encouraged to make proper presents. A
woman, by clever speech and prudent action, can get a good
ham from one, and a roll of cloth from another; and make still
another give poultry or wine. But this poor dumb thing,
Catherine, gets nothing at all. While my fellow-judges have
their kitchens and cellars and stables and storerooms running
over with good things, all thanks to their wives, I hardly get
wherewithal to keep the pot boiling. You see, Master Adam
Fumée, what I lose by having a dumb wife. I'm not worth half
as much….And the worst of it, is, I'm losing my spirits, and
almost my wits, with it all.

Thirst

Eugene O'Neill
1913–14

Scene: a steamer's life raft, rising and falling slowly on the long ground swell of a glassy tropic sea

Dramatic
Gentleman: a former first-class passenger on the steamer, 30–40

The gentleman has survived the steamer's sinking along with two other shipmates. Here, he describes his experience to a woman who was a dancer and to a man who was one of the deck hands.

GENTLEMAN: *(In a dead voice.)* You were very beautiful. I was looking at you and wondering what kind of a woman you were. You know I had never met you personally—only seen you in my walks around the deck. Then came the crash—that horrible dull crash. We were all thrown forward on the floor of the salon; then screams, oaths, fainting women, the hollow boom of a bulkhead giving way. I vaguely remember rushing to my state-room and picking up my wallet. It must have been that menu that I took instead. Then I was on deck fighting in the midst of the crowd. Somehow I got into a boat—but it was overloaded and was swamped immediately. I swam to another boat. They beat me off with the oars. That boat too was swamped a moment later. And then the gurgling, choking cries of the drowning! Something huge rushed by me in the water, leaving a gleaming trail of phosphorescence. A woman near me with a life belt around her gave a cry of agony and disappeared—then I realized—sharks! I became frenzied with terror. I swam. I beat the water with my hands. The ship had gone down. I swam and swam with but one idea—to put all that horror behind me. I saw something white on the water before me. I clutched it—climbed on it. It was this raft. You and he were on it. I fainted. The whole thing is a horrible nightmare in my brain—but I remember clearly that idiotic remark of the woman in the salon. What pitiful creatures we are!

Ulysses
Stephen Phillips
1902

Scene: Ithaca

Dramatic
Ulysses: the wandering hero, 40s

When finally deposited on the shores of his beloved Ithaca,
Ulysses thinks himself to be dreaming.

ULYSSES: Slowly the mist fades! Ah! the cypress tree
I was so proud to plant as a boy! and there
The cave forbidden which I therefore loved!
Brighter, more bright! The crest of Neriton!
The rustling glade there where I killed the boar.
Now all the land gleams; look you there! the ridge
Where the young laughing babe Telemachus
First clapped his hands at sight of the sea: and O!
Yon holy winding path where last I kissed
Penelope, who toward me swayed and spoke not.
I came there down the slope most lingeringly,
And turned by the myrtle tree, and turned and turned.
Goddess, I cannot see for the great tears.
There! there! the very peak to which she climbed
Waving a sea-farewell with helpless hands!
O verdure to the seaman that's come home!
O light upon the land where I was born!
O dear, dear Earth, thou warm mother of me,
Art glad, art glad in thy brown bosom; here
I kiss and kiss thee; here I fling me down
And roll and clasp and cover me with thee!
(Starting up.)
Ah! 'tis a dream: O God, it is a lure!
Incredible that ever I can rest!
I am fooled by the old sea-magic; my home trembles;
An apparition of the glassy deep,
A fading island that we come to never!
Is it rooted, rooted fast and cannot fly?
I shall go mad if I am fooled! Speak! speak!
Is this the earth, the earth where I was born?

The Zykovs

Maxim Gorky, Trans. by Alexander Bakshy
1914

Scene: Russia

Dramatic
Antipa Zykov: a ruthless businessman, 50s

When he is chastised by his idealistic young wife for not loving his own son, Zykov reveals the heartless philosophy with which he has governed his life.

ANTIPA: Is it my fault I'm in better health? Is it my fault I don't feel sorry for those who are good-for-nothing? I love business. I love work. On whose bones has this world been built? Whose sweat and blood have watered the earth? That hasn't been done by the likes of him and you. Can he take upon himself the work I do? (…)
Hundreds of people live without want, hundreds have come up in the world, thanks to my work and my father's before me. What has he done? I did something wrong, but at least I'm always working toward some end. To listen to you kindhearted people, every kind of work is a sin against something. That's not true. My father used to say, if you don't kill poverty you don't wash away sin, and that's the truth.

American Buffalo

David Mamet

1976

Scene: a junk shop

Serio-Comic
Teach: an ordinary guy, 40–50

Here, Teach complains about the behavior of Ruthie, a
woman who recently beat him at cards.

TEACH: I come into the Riverside to get a cup of *coffee,* right? I sit
down at the table with Gracie and Ruthie. (…)
I'm gonna order just a cup of coffee. (…)
So Grace and Ruthie's having breakfast, and they're done.
Plates…crusts of stuff all over…So we'll shoot the shit. (…)
Talk about the *game…* (…)
…*so* on. Down I sit. "Hi, hi" I take a piece of toast off Grace's
plate… (…)
…and she goes "Help yourself." Help myself. I should help
myself to half a piece of toast it's four slices for a quarter. I
should have a nickel every time we're over at the game, I pop
for coffee…cigarettes…a *sweet roll,* never say a word. "Bobby,
see who wants what." Huh? A fucking *roast-beef* sandwich.
Am I right? Ahh, shit. We're sitting down, how many times do I
pick up the check? But (No!) because I never go and make a big
thing out of it—it's no big thing—and flaunt like "This one's on
me" like some bust-out asshole, but I naturally assume that I'm
with friends, and don't forget who's who when someone gets
behind a half a yard or needs some help with (huh?) some fucking rent, or drops enormous piles of money at the track, or
someone's *sick* or something… (…)
Only (and I tell you this, Don). Only, and I'm not, I don't think,
casting anything on anyone: from the mouth of a Southern
bulldyke asshole ingrate of a vicious nowhere cunt can this
trash come. And I take nothing back, and I know you're close
with them. (…)
I have always treated everybody more than fair, and never gone

around complaining. (…)

Someone is *against* me, that's their problem…I can look our for myself, and I don't got to fuck around behind somebody's back, I don't like the way they're treating me. (Or pray some brick *safe* falls and hits them on the head, they're walking down the street.) But to have that shithead turn, in one breath, every fucking sweet roll that I ever ate with them into *ground glass* (I'm wondering were they eating it and thinking "This guy's an idiot to blow a fucking *quarter* on his friends"…) …this hurts me, Don. This hurts me in a way I don't know what the fuck to do.

The Birthday Party

Harold Pinter
1958

Scene: a house in a seaside resort town

Dramatic
Goldberg: a sinister man, 50s

*Goldberg and McCann have mysteriously appeared at a
boarding house, their intent unclear. Here, Goldberg boasts
of his good health before suffering a brief breakdown.*

GOLDBERG: Wait! *(He stretches his arms to the arms of the chair.)*
Come here. I want your opinion. Have a look in my mouth. *(He
opens his mouth wide.)* Take a good look. You know what I
mean? You know what? I've never lost a tooth. Not since the
day I was born. Nothing's changed. *(He gets up.)* That's why I've
reached my position, McCann. Because I've always been as fit
as a fiddle. All my life I've said the same. Play up, play up, and
play the game. Honour thy father and thy mother. All along the
line. Follow the line, the line, McCann, and you can't go wrong.
What do you think, I'm a self-made man? No! I sat where I was
told to sit. I kept my eye on the ball. School? Don't talk to me
about school. Top in all subjects. And for why? Because I'm
telling you, I'm telling you, follow my line? Follow my mental?
Learn by heart. Never write down a thing. No. And don't go too
near the water. And you'll find—that what I say is true.
Because I believe that the world… *(Vacant.)*
Because I believe that the world… *(Desperate)* …
Because I believe that the world… *(Lost.)* …
(He sits in chair.) Sit down, McCann, sit here where I can look at
you. *(Intensely, with growing certainty.)* My father said to me,
Benny, Benny, he said, come here. He was dying. I knelt down.
By him day and night. Who else was there? Forgive, Benny, he
said, and let live. Yes, Dad. Go home to your wife. I will, Dad.
Keep an eye open for low-lives, for schnorrers and for
layabouts. He didn't mention names. I lost my life in the service
of others, he said, I'm not ashamed. Do your duty and keep

your observations. Always bid good morning to the neighbours. Never, never forget your family, for they are the rock, the constitution and the core! If you're ever in any difficulties Uncle Barney will see you in the clear. I knelt down. *(He kneels.)* I swore on the good book. And I knew the word I had to remember—Respect! Because McCann— *(Gently.)* Seamus—who came before your father? His father. And who came before him? Before him? *(Vacant—triumphant.)* Who came before your father's father out your father's father's mother! Your great-gran-granny. *(Silence. He slowly rises.)* And that's why I've reached my position, McCann. Because I've always been as fit as a fiddle. My motto. Work hard and play hard. Not a day's illness.

The Boy Who Ate the Moon

Jane Martin
1981

Scene: the waiting room at a doctor's office

Dramatic
James: a young man in need of medical attention 18–20

*James is convinced that he has swallowed the moon. Here,
he describes the result.*

JAMES: Last night I could see my hands in the dark. It suddenly
occurred to me that I was going to ignite. I think it must be very
painful to burn…I mean that's different from heat. I would be
very afraid to burn… (…)
Remember how they taught you that by rubbing two
sticks…well that's…my inside rubs against my outside. It was
raining last night so I figured it would put me out. I went
out…went out in the rain and down by the laundromat…down
by Spring Street there was a pool and the moon…I was pretty
sure that if the rain on the outside, the outside of me
didn't…well then I'd just drink the water…put me out that
way…but I wasn't…you know…thinking clearly and I…and I
swallowed the moon. Well just the beginning of one…part of a
moon. It's going to grow inside me…you know…for however
many days…making pressure…making me hotter…I'm uh…I'm
uh going to leak flame…I'm pretty sure it will set me on
fire…you know, in my condition…see the thing is that once you
start getting hot it's really hard to cool down.

The Captivity of Pixie Shedman

Romulus Linney

1986

Scene: a studio in a New York City hotel, August 1962

Dramatic
Dr. Shedman: an alcoholic in exile, 40s

Shedman has married his father's mistress, Pixie. In order to avoid a scandal, they move to a remote corner of Kansas where Pixie turns to poetry and Shedman to booze. Here, the drunken doctor reads one of Pixie's poems and confesses that he's having an affair.

DR. SHEDMAN: All right. *(Doctor Shedman looks at the poem again.)* We'll continue. *(Reading.)* "The heart that through the toilsome day Beat high with hope—" Oops! The title! Right there smack in the middle of the poem. Oh, very good. *(Reading.)* "The heart that through the toilsome day Beat high with hope—on rugged away. Above the strife of worldly gain With faith serene, is filled with pain." Oh, dear me. Pixie filled with pain. No, the heart filled with pain, sorry. After beating through the toilsome day, high with hope. You know, I think it has to be one or the other, but let it pass. It's strong and sensitive, and of course above the strife of worldly gain, otherwise it wouldn't be poetic, would it? (…)
(Reading.) "High winds of stress and low'ring clouds. Obscuring mists—" Well, I think I know what you're talking about there— "Through darkness, maze, from crushing blow His hand will hold, give—" Wait a minute. His hand? Who's his? A mysterious intruder? Don Juan? Almighty God? The mailman? Well, we just have to guess, and that's poetic, too. All right. *(Reading.)* "His hand will hold, give faith to grow, Through pall of gloom, a joy again, Still sweeter after wind and rain." Rain, a-gain. The subtlety of it meets one at every turn. *(He stands looking at her, weaving a little, and smiling.)* Well, let me tell you this. I do sympathize with all this pain you're in, but we've been married four years now, and I'm in a little discomfort myself. Lacking the tongue of the poet, I just go dancing, like any clod, to kill my

pain. And, like any clod, I have a drink, or two or three or four, with other clods. One such is a waitress at the Starlight Cafe in Hazleton. You wouldn't like her. She drinks, too. Not only that, she dances. Worst of all, the little girl's pregnant. And you know what, Pixie? Here's a couplet for you. "She won't be quiet, she'll cause a fuss. She's just going to try and blame it on us!" And you know something else? I don't care. Because my little waitress doesn't pretend to be something she isn't. She just likes to work, dance, drink and you-know-what. She doesn't mope around like Little Eva, and brood around like Lady Macbeth, and make me feel like a goddamned dog with a lot of goddamned doggerel!

Dejavu
John Osborne
1992

Scene: the Midlands

Serio-Comic
JP: a man whose life has passed him by, 50–60

*JP is the older version of "Jimmy," who first appeared in
Osborne's* Look Back in Anger. *Thirty years older, JP appears
no wiser as he here reveals.*

JP: No. I don't know much less than I do about my children, their
mother. My ex-wife. I look for a glimpse of pleasure not enlight-
enment. Look at Teddy, he's quite a jolly little sphinx if you've a
whimsical bent. But his secret's not worth the probing. I've
looked for secrets where there were none. Everyone demands
solutions, like happiness, as their right. You go to sleep at night
and wake up with the same old *Giaconda* frown beside you.
(Sings to the tune 'Amapola':)
    Giaconda, my smiling Giaconda,
    I like to watch and wonder,
    I know I'll never get beyond its empty mystery.
I thought my first wife was concealing something. Something to
declare *there,* I thought. Now she does, of course. To the whole
world. Like Janey Proudfoot. I've no secrets. But I'm sometimes
in the market for them. Like old T. Bear there. That's why he
keeps changing his dumb little mind and it runs ever the same.
Well, this won't buy the baby a new bonnet.
    Replete of sin, devoid of guilt,
    For holocaust I never built
    A cheery, unrepentant sod,
    Mine's an ad hoc relationship with God.

Edmond

David Mamet
1982

Scene: a prison cell

Dramatic
Edmond: a man suspected of murder, 30–40

*Edmond has been jailed for killing a girl. Here, he is visited
by his wife who asks him whether or not he committed the
crime. His response reveals more than a simple confession.*

EDMOND: You want to tell me you're *mad* at me or something? (…)
[Yes,] but I want to tell you something…I didn't mean to. But
do you want to hear something *funny?*…(Now don't laugh….) I
think I'd just had too much coffee. *(Pause.)* I'll tell you something else: I think there are just too many people in the world. I
think that's why we kill each other. *(Pause.)* I…I…I suppose
you're mad at me for leaving you. *(Pause.)* I don't suppose
you're, uh, inclined (or, nor do I think you should be) to stand
by me. I understand that. *(Pause.)* I'm sure that there are mar-
riages where the wife would. Or the husband if it would go
that way. *(Pause.)* But I know ours is not one of that type.
(Pause.) I know that you *wished* at one point it would be. I
wished that too. At one point. *(Pause.)* I know at certain times
we wished we could be…closer to each other. I can say that
now. I'm sure this is the way you feel when someone near you
dies. You never said the things you wanted desperately to say. It
would have been so simple to say them. *(Pause.)* But you never
did.

Edmond

David Mamet

1982

Scene: a prison cell

Dramatic
Edmond: a man suspected of murder, 30–40

Here Edmond lashes out angrily at the prison chaplain.

EDMOND: Oh. Nothing is impossible. Not to "God," is that what
you're saying? (…)
Well, then, you're full of *shit.* You understand that. If nothing's
impossible to God, then let him let me walk *out* of here and be
free. Let him cause a new *day.* In a perfect land full of *life.* And
air. Where people are *kind* to each other, and there's *work* to
do. Where we grow up in *love,* and in security we're *wanted.*
(Pause.) Let him do that. Let him. Tell him to do that. *(Pause.)*
You asshole—if nothing's impossible…I think *that* must be
easy…Not: "Let me *fly,*" or, "If there is a God make him to
make the *sun* come out at night." Go on. Please. Please. Please.
I'm *begging* you. If you're so smart. Let him do that: Let him do
that. *(Pause.)* Please. *(Pause.)* Please. I'm begging you.

The End of the Day
Jon Robin Baitz
1992

Scene: Los Angeles

Dramatic
Graydon Massey: a frustrated doctor, 40–50

Massey, an ex-patriot Brit, has given up his lucrative Beverly Hills psychiatric practice to run the oncology department of an impoverished clinic. The dire conditions in the clinic prove to be more than he can cope with, however, leading him to clash with the clinic's director.

MASSEY: And do you imagine, you self-righteous, impotent little do-gooder, that you've ever been of any assistance to any of these people? Because this isn't a hospital—*nothing works!* In a real hospital, people come in sick and leave better. In a real hospital, someone can get a splint, an aspirin, a band-aid. In a real hospital, there are stitches. In a real hospital, there are orderlies. Not rivers of plasma and vomit and just three Trinidadian residents who can't tell the difference between measles, smallpox and sarcoma. So please don't lecture me on being here until you find a way to run this place competently! Instead of lording over the sick so as to feel better as they pop off. You're worse than I am, lady, because you know *precisely* what you're doing and—even more—contemptibly—you know what you *should* be doing. Which makes you nothing so much as a ghoulish little commandant, Dr. Mengele's bookkeeper!

Epitaph for George Dillon

John Osborne and Anthony Creighton
1958

Scene: the home of the Elliot family just outside London

Serio-Comic
George Dillon: a failed playwright, 30s

When the woman he loves prepares to leave him, George bitterly offers her his "epitaph."

GEORGE: Listen! I'll make you laugh yet, before you go. Just a trip on the stage-cloth, and Lear teeters on, his crown around his ears, his grubby tights full of moth-holes. How they all long for those tights to fall down. What a relief it would be! Oh, we should all use stronger elastic. And the less sure we are of our pathetic little divine rights, the stronger the elastic we should use. You've seen the whole, shabby, solemn pretence now. This is where you came in. For God's sake go. (…)
No, wait. Shall I recite my epitaph to you? Yes, do recite your epitaph to me. Here lies the body of George Dillon, aged thirty-four—or thereabouts—who thought, who hoped, he was that mysterious, ridiculous being called an artist. He never allowed himself one day of peace. He worshipped the physical things of this world, and was betrayed by his own body. He loved also the things of the mind, but his own brain was a cripple from the waist down. He achieved nothing he set out to do. He made no one happy, no one looked up with excitement when he entered the room. He was always troubled with wind round his heart, but he loved no one successfully. He was a bit of a bore, and, frankly, rather useless. But the germs loved him. Even his sentimental epitaph is probably a pastiche of someone or other, but he doesn't quite know who. And, in the end, it doesn't really matter.

For Whom the Southern Belle Tolls

Christopher Durang
1993

Scene: a southern home

Serio-Comic
Tom: a sensitive southerner, 20–30

*Tom could no longer bear to live with his nagging mother
and alcoholic brother, so he finally left home as he here
relates.*

TOM: I didn't go to the moon, I went to the movies. In Amsterdam.
A long, lonely trip working my way on a freighter. They had
good movies in Amsterdam. They weren't in English, but I didn't
really care. And as for my mother and brother—well they were
impossible to live with, so I didn't miss them. Or so I thought.
For something pursued me. It always came upon me unawares,
it always caught me by surprise. Sometimes it would be a swizzle stick in someone's vodka glass, or sometimes it would just
be a jar of pigs feet. But then all of a sudden my brother touches my shoulder, and my mother puts her hands around my
neck, and everywhere I look I am reminded of them. And in all
the bars I go to there are those damn swizzle sticks everywhere.
I find myself thinking of my brother Lawrence. And of his collection of glass. And of my mother. I begin to think that their story
would maybe make a good novel, or even a play. A mother's
hopes, a brother's dreams. Pathos, humor, even tragedy. But
then I lose interest, I really haven't the energy. So I'll leave them
both, dimly lit, in my memory. For nowadays the world is lit by
lightning; and when we get those colored lights going, it feels
like I'm on LSD. Or some other drug. Or maybe it's the trick of
memory, or the memory of some trick. Play with your cocktail
stirrers, Lawrence. And so, good-bye.

Gemini

Albert Innaurato
1978

Scene: a neighborhood in Philadelphia, 1973

Serio-Comic
Fran Geminiani: a boisterous, friendly working-class dad, 45

Here, Fran offers his Harvard-bound son some advice about women.

FRAN: Well, Lucille had a fight wit Aunt Emma. That's why we came
back. It was over water bugs. I didn't see no water bugs. But
Lucille said they was everywhere. Aunt Emma thought she was
accusin' her of bein' dirty. So we came back. (…)
She's good people, she means well. There ain't nothin' like a
woman's company, remember that, my son, there ain't nothin'
like a woman. You can think there is. I thought the horses was
just as good; hell, I thought the horses was better. But I was
wrong. But you gotta be careful of white women. I guess us
dagos go afta them; hell, I went afta you mother, and she was
white as this Judith, though not near as pretty. But you gotta be
careful of them kinda women. A white woman's like a big hole,
you can never be sure what's in there. So you be careful, even if
she is a Italian major. What do you want for your birthday
tomorrow?

Imperceptible Mutibilities in the Third Kingdom

Suzi Lori Parks
1989

Scene: here and now

Dramatic
Smith: a military man reunited with his family, 40–50

Here, Smith describes his desire to have done something noble.

SMITH: Always wanted to do me somethin noble. Not somethin better than what I deserved—just somethin noble. Uh little bit uh noble somethin. Like what they did in thuh olden days. Like in thuh olden days in olden wars. Time for noble seems past. Time for somethin noble was yesterday. There usta be uh overlap of four hours. Hours in four when I'd say "today" and today itd be. Them four hours usta happen together, now, they scatters theirselves all throughout thuh day. Usta be uh flap tuh slip through. Flaps gone shut. I saw that boy fallin out thuh sky. On fire. Thought he was uh star. Uh star that died years uhgo but was givin us light through thuh flap. Made uh wish. Opened up my arms—was wishin for my whole family. He fell on me. They saw he was flyin too close to thuh sun. They say I caught him but he fell. On me. They gived me uh distinction. They set me apart. They say I caught him but he fell. He fell on me. I broked his fall. I saved his life. I ain't seen him since. No, boy—Duffy—uh—Muffy, Buffy, no, we ain't even turtls. Huh. We'se slugs. Slugs. Slugs.

Jack and Jill

Jane Martin
1995

Scene: here and now

serio-comic
Jack: 20s–30s

Here, Jack reacts to being described as "nice."

JACK: Goddamnit! Goddamnit!! *(During monologue, Jack removes sports coat and tosses it offstage. Later, he removes shirt and tosses it offstage.)* Nice, right? Nice. Okay. One second. One second. This nice we are talking about here..."don't be nice, Jack." This "nice" has a bad name...to say the goddamn least. Women, to generalize, hate nice...no, no, they like it in clerks, they like it in auto mechanics...but...nice guys finish last, right? Why? Because "nice" is essentially thought to lack complexity, mystery. "Nice" just...has no sex appeal...it just doesn't understand the situation. Women distrust "nice" because, given the cultural context, they themselves can't possibly *be* nice. How can the powerless be "nice." What good is nice to the "exploited?" So women loathe nice because they see, they know what a phony mask it is in their own lives, so when they perceive it in a man it just pisses them off. What they prefer are abusive qualities moderated by charm, because they are already abused personalities, given the culture. I'm not kidding. Hey, I don't buy it because there is another "nice," a hard-won, complex, covered-with-blood-and-gore "nice." An existential, steel willed, utterly crucial and necessary "nice" that says to the skags in the motorcycle gang, "Fuck you and the hogs you rode in on. I exemplify hope and reason and concern." See, I raise the fallen banner high, Jill, so satirize me, shoot me, stab me, dismiss me, go screw the Four Horsemen of the Apocalypse if that's what turns you on, *I'm nice!! (He slowly turns back into himself.)* Sorry, I didn't, uh...don't know how I got into that...just "nice," you know...well, anyway, sorry.

Look Back in Anger

John Osborne
1956

Scene: a one-room flat in the Midlands

Dramatic
Jimmy: a miserable and sometimes abusive young man, 25

*Jimmy's enjoyment of a radio concert is diminished by the
sounds made by his wife, who is ironing. Here, he cruelly
describes the clumsiness of women.*

JIMMY: Don't try and patronize me. *(Turning to Cliff.)* She's so clumsy.
I watch for her to do the same things every night. The way she
jumps on the bed, as if she were stamping on someone's face,
and draws the curtains back with a great clatter, in that casually
destructive way of hers. It's like someone launching a battleship.
Have you ever noticed how noisy women are? Have you? The
way they kick the floor about, simply walking over it? Or have
you watched them sitting at their dressing tables, dropping their
weapons and banging down their bits of boxes and brushes
and lipsticks? I've watched her doing it night after night. When
you see a woman in front of her bedroom mirror, you realize
what a refined sort of a butcher she is. Did you ever see some
dirty old Arab, sticking his fingers into some mess of lamb fat
and gristle? Well, she's just like that. Thank God they don't have
many women surgeons! Those primitive hands would have your
guts out in no time. Flip! Out it comes, like the powder out of
its box. Flop! Back it goes, like the power puff on the table.
(…)
She'd drop your guts like hair clips and fluff all over the floor.
You've got to be fundamentally insensitive to be as noisy and as
clumsy as that. I had a flat underneath a couple of girls once.
You heard every damned thing those bastards did, all day and
night. The most simple, everyday actions were a sort of assault
course on your sensibilities. I used to plead with them. I even
got to screaming the most ingenious obscenities I could think
of, up the stairs at them. But nothing, nothing, would move

them. With those two, even a simple visit to the lavatory sounded like a medieval siege. Oh, they beat me in the end—I had to go. I expect they're still at it. Or they're probably married by now, and driving some other poor devils out of their minds. Slamming their doors, stamping their high heels, banging their irons and saucepans—the eternal flaming racket of the female.

Look Back in Anger

John Osborne
1956

Scene: a one-room flat in the Midlands

Dramatic
Jimmy: a miserable and sometimes abusive young man, 25

Here, Jimmy lashes out at Alison, his long-suffering wife, whose upper-class upbringing has always been a thorn in his side.

JIMMY: Oh, my dear wife, you've got so much to learn. I only hope you learn it one day. If only something—something would happen to you, and wake you out of your beauty sleep! If you could have a child, and it would die. Let it grow, let a recognizable human face emerge from that little mass of indiarubber and wrinkles. Please—if only I could watch you face that. I wonder if you might even become a recognizable human being yourself. But I doubt it. Do you know I have never known the great pleasure of lovemaking when I didn't desire it myself. Oh, it's not that she hasn't her own kind of passion. She has the passion of a python. She just devours me whole every time, as if I were some over-large rabbit. That's me. That bulge around her navel—if you're wondering what it is—it's me. Me, buried alive down there, and going mad, smothered in that peaceful looking coil. Not a sound, not a flicker from her—she doesn't even rumble a little. You'd think that this indigestible mess would stir up some kind of tremor in these distended, overfed tripes—but not her! She'll go on sleeping and devouring until there's nothing left of me.

Middle-Aged White Guys

Jane Martin
1994

Scene: a dump

Serio-Comic
Elvis: a cosmic messenger, 40s

Here, the King returns to Earth to inspire White Anglo-Saxon men to wake up and achieve their true potential.

ELVIS: I'm the King of the White Man, asshole [who are you?] (…)
The Velvet Rocker, buddy, the Hillbilly Cat, the King of Western Bop. (…)
I been dinin' on cumulus Nimbus. (…)
[Well, I'm not dressed up as a Smith Brothers cough drop.] I'll tell y'all one thing, boys, there wasn't nobody, nowhere, no time, no way, ever seen a white boy move like me. They couldn't shake it where I shook it or take it where I took it. I was born with a guitar in one hand and the ruination of western civilization in the other. Y'all look a little tight there, boys, so the King's gotta' get you ready to party! Heck, have some Dexedrine… *(He scatters hundreds of pills in a multi-colored spray from his pockets as if they were coins for the multitudes.)* Have some Tuinal, Dilaudid, Quaaludes and Demerol! Get up, or get down, get wherever you need to be to hear the *word!* (…) Uh-huh! Hit it! The Lord, she stood on the rim of the universe, and she did regard the earth, baby. And wherever her gaze did fall there was real bad doody goin' down. There was a sickly caste, a dread pigmentless, soulless, milky pale fungi suckin' the sustenance right out of the world, man, leavin' things undone, done badly, overlooked, overgrazed, snafued and skimmin' the cream right off the top. And who the hell was in the driver's seat takin' care of business? Buddy, it was a bunch of fat old white men, that's who it was! Greedy ol' farts livin' off the fat of the land while the land fell apart in their hands. They weren't gettin' it there, dudes! You can't rhumba in a sports car, baby. You can't do no Australian crawl in a shot glass. We had it,

man, and we pissed it away! Regard me, brethren. I was the most beautiful cat ever rolled into Memphis in a '39 Plymouth. I could sing black boogie and the Mississippi Delta blues. I could shuck and jive like a funky angel. I was the white man triumphant, baby. If I wanted it *now*, I got it *now*. I was the boss, the king, El Presidente Grande, and I ended up fat as a grain-fed hog, down on my knees on the bathroom floor with my head floatin' in a toilet bowl. Hell, you're down in the bowl with me, boys. Y'all had played errorless, no-hit ball goin' into the eighth inning, and you took it from there to the dung heap, poisoned in spirit and your women flee you into the night with whatever they can carry.

The Road to Mecca

Athol Fugard
1984

Scene: New Bethesda, South Africa, 1974

Dramatic
Marius Byleveld: a well-meaning Dominee, 60s

*Here, Marius pays a visit to an eccentric parishioner, Miss
Helen, whom he tries to entertain with a tale of his inspiration for an upcoming sermon.*

MARIUS: *(A little laugh.)* Relax, Helen. I only said "thanks to you"
because it came to me this afternoon while I was digging up
your vegetables. I spent a lot of time, while I was out in the garden doing that, just leaning on my spade. My back is giving me
a bit of trouble again and, to tell you the truth, I also felt lazy. I
wasn't thinking about anything in particular…just looking, you
know, the way an old man does, looking around, recognizing
once again and saying the names. Spitskop in the distance!
Aasvoelkrans down at the other end of the valley. The poplars
with their autumn foliage standing around as yellow and still as
that candle flame! And a lot of remembering. As you know,
Helen, I had deep and very painful wounds in my soul when I
first came here. Wounds I thought would never heal. This was
going to be where I finally escaped from life, turned my back
on it and justified what was left of my existence by ministering
to you people's simple needs. I was very wrong. I didn't escape
life here, I discovered it, what it really means, the fullness and
goodness of it. It's a deep and lasting regret that Aletta wasn't
alive to share that discovery with me. Anyway, all of this was
going on in my head when I realized I was hearing a small little
voice, and the small little voice was saying, "Thank you." With
every spadeful of earth that I turned when I went down on my
knees to lift the potatoes out of the soil, there it was: "Thank
you." It was mine! I was muttering away to myself the way we
old folks are inclined to do when nobody is around. It was me
saying, "Thank you." That is what I want to do tomorrow,

Helen. Give thanks, but in a way that I've never done before. I know I've stood there in the pulpit many times telling all of you to do exactly that, but oh dear me, the cleverness and conceit in the soul of Marius Byleveld when he was doing that! I had an actor's vanity up there, Helen. I'm not saying I was a total hypocrite but, believe me, in those thanksgivings I was listening to my dominee's voice and its hoped-for eloquence every bit as much as to the true little voice inside my heart...the voice I heard so clearly this afternoon. That's the voice that must speak tomorrow! And to do that I must find words as simple as the sky I was standing under this afternoon or the earth I was turning over with my spade. They have got no vanities and conceits. They are just "there." If the Almighty takes pity on us, the one gives us rain so that the other can in turn...give us this day our daily potato. *(A smile at this gentle little joke.)* Am I making sense, Helen? Answer me truthfully.

The Substance of Fire

Jon Robin Baitz
1990

Scene: New York City, the present

Dramatic
Isaac: a floundering publisher trying to reconcile his past
through the works he publishes, 60–70

When Isaac refuses to publish what will certainly be a popular book, he is confronted by his three children who all own stock in the company. They proceed to express concern for his recent interest in publishing Holocaust-related material and threaten to take over the company with their collective shares. His back against the wall, Isaac here reveals something about his obsession with the Holocaust just before firing his oldest son.

ISAAC: I spent a couple of days, a little boy, wandering about after the liberation. I saw a particular kind of man—a wraith-like figure—who could only have been in the camps. But with a brown pinstripe suit, a fleur-de-lis on his tie and manicured nails, trying to pick up where he left off, as if you could. I never say anything about this. Why talk? Why bother? I wasn't in the camps. You know? They're busy throwing the Farbers and the Hirsches into the ovens, and I'm happily eating smoked eels in the basement, with my Stendahl and Dumas. What did I know? I was protected, sheltered by my cousins. And then I got out of the basement and into the wrecked world. I came to this country. You re-invent yourself. Make it as a bon vivant in Manhattan. Meet this woman—this extraordinary woman. Marry. Have these kids. Go to so many cocktail parties, host so many more…and they…haunt. *(Beat.)* I have kept my eyes closed to the world outside the basement for so long. The wrecked world all around us. But I can no longer close my eyes. *(He turns to Aaron.)* My son. You are fired. I will give you a week to clear your desk, and I will give you letters of recommendation. But I will not speak to you, I will not communicate with you, I will not… *(Pause.)* …give at all. Kiddo. To the victor go the spoils.

The Substance of Fire

Jon Robin Baitz
1990

Scene: New York City, the present

Dramatic
Isaac: a floundering publisher trying to reconcile his past
through the works he publishes, 60–70

*Three years later the company has gone bankrupt and
Isaac's children are trying to have him committed. Here,
Isaac reveals his feelings about his children to the social
worker sent to evaluate his case.*

ISAAC: You can't even imagine. You have no idea. This is not how I
saw my life turn out. But surprised I am not, Miss Hackett. I did
this to myself? You don't see any other survivors in your files,
do you? You don't see any brothers and sisters? Betrayal? I
never even smelt it coming until the fucking *maid* turned us in.
The *maid*. She was like my mother, and let me tell you—I don't
have self-pity! You don't see a tattoo on my wrist, do you? But
they got my grandparents, they got my mother and father, and
they got...I came here to make a family and they trashed it,
they got it. (...)
Listen to me. You came here with an agenda, but now at least
listen to what was taken away from me. *(Pause.)* I loved my children. I sure don't love them now. You walk into this house...
(He points to a table.) Aaron cut his head on the tip of that
table and I carried him to NYU Hospital when he was two.
(Beat.) Sarah got laid for the first time in this house, and I
thought I was quite literally going to die. *(Beat.)* My wife found
this sofa in Kingston and we had it carted down and we sat on
it, and it was the most perfect...my wife...my wife...my wife.
(Beat.) My Martin. He comes in here from Lacrosse when he
was sixteen, sneezing, and the next thing, he was, just like
that—no blood count at all. *(Beat.)* I sleep now in the living
room, because the bedrooms are too much to bear. *(Beat.)* I am
so stupid, Miss Hackett, I thought that if I published Hazlitt and
Svevo, I'd be spared. The silence, Miss Hackett. The silence.
Pointless.

The Taking of Miss Janie

Ed Bullins

1974

Scene: California, the 60s

Dramatic
Monty: a black college student with a street background, 20s

Here, Monty analyzes Janie's interest in him.

MONTY: *(Smokes a joint.)* This white chick, Janie, thinks she's got my nose open. Thinks she's stringin' me along. But I got news for her. She treats me like this cause I'm black. Who does she think she is? I'm as good, nawh, better than any white dude she could have. Really, I'm doin' this girl a favor by payin' some attention to her. Look at all the broads around me. Peggy...Flossy...I bet I could even have Sharon if Len didn't go for her. But I don't cut into my buddies' chicks. All I got to do is snap my fingers and I could have almost any woman I wanted. So why should I get my guts tied up in knots about this blond fake. She's nothin' but a tease. Says she likes my poetry. Tell me now, how could a white broad love "Down with Whitey," poetry? Tells me she loves my mind. Haaa...I wouldn't have much of a mind if I believed her. She came to my party, the one where I invited her, and told her corny little boyfriend where she'd be. Who does she think she is? She can't make a fool out of me. She's mine even if she doesn't know it yet! And I'm gonna take her when I'm ready. And the time's right. That's right, get her. Take her, get her, have her...whatever I gotta do. I dig her blond lookin' self. And I don't care how long it takes to get her. I got all the time in the world. 'Cause the world is what you make it.

Tango

Slawomir Mrozek, Trans. by Ralph Manheim
& Teresa Dzieduscycka
1965

Scene: an apartment in Poland

Dramatic
Stromil: a patriarch dedicated to the principles of revolution,
50s

*When his son complains of the repressive life they're forced
to live under the regime created by revolution, Stromil
angrily reminds him that life before the change was intolerable.*

STROMIL: [Unfortunately?] You don't know what you're saying. If
you'd lived in those days, you'd know how much we've done
for you. You have no idea what the world was like then. Can
you imagine how much courage it took to dance the tango? Do
you realize that in those days there were hardly any fallen
women? That the only recognized style of painting was natural-
ism? That the theater was utterly bourgeois? Stifling.
Insufferable. You couldn't even put your elbows down on the
dinner table! I can still remember a youth demonstration on
that very issue. Why, it wasn't until after 1900 that the boldest,
the most advanced spirits stopped giving up their seats to elder-
ly people. No, we didn't spare ourselves in our struggle for
these rights and if you today can push your grandmother
around, its to us your thanks are due. You simply can't imagine
how much you owe us. To think how we struggled to give you
this freedom which you now despise!

Tango

Slawomir Mrozek, Trans. by Ralph Manheim
& Teresa Dzieduscycka
1965

Scene: an apartment in Poland

Dramatic
Arthur: a passionate young man, 25

*Arthur is committed to changing his repressive world, and
the first step in his agenda is to reintroduce church weddings. Here, he proposes to the woman his thinks he loves.*

ARTHUR: Marry me. That's the first step. No more promiscuity, no
more *dolce vita*. A real marriage. Not just dropping into city hall
between breakfast and lunch. A genuine old-fashioned wedding
with an organ playing and bridesmaids marching down the
aisle. I'm especially counting on the procession. It will take them
by surprise. That's the whole idea. And, from then on, they
won't have time to think, to organize resistance and spread
defeatism. It's the first shot that counts. Catching them off
guard like that, we can force them to accept conventions they'll
never break out of again. It's going to be the kind of wedding
they'll have to take part in, and on my terms. I'll turn them into
a bridal procession, and at long last my father will be forced to
button his fly. What do you say? (...) [White as snow.]
Everything strictly according to the rules. And at the same time
you'll be helping all the women in the world. The rebirth of
convention will set them free. What used to be the first rule of
every encounter between a man and a woman? Conversation.
A man couldn't get what he wanted just by making inarticulate
sounds. He couldn't just grunt, he had to talk. And while he
was talking, you—the woman—sat there demurely, sizing your
opponent up. You let him talk and he showed his hand.
Listening serenely, you drew up your own order of battle.
Observing his tactics, you planned your own accordingly. Free to
maneuver, you were always in command of the situation. You
had time to think before coming to a decision and you could
drag things out as long as you wanted. Even if he gnashed his

teeth and secretly wished you in the bottom of hell, you knew he would never dare hit you. Up to the very last minute you could move freely, securely, triumphantly. Once you were engaged, you were safe, and even then traditional avenues of escape were open to you. Such were the blessings of conversation! But nowadays? Nowadays a man doesn't even have to introduce himself—and you will admit it's handy to know who a man is and what he does for a living.

Waiting for Godot

Samuel Beckett
1952

Scene: a country road, a tree

Serio-Comic
Vladimir: a man waiting, any age

Here, Vladimir assures his companions that they are doing the right thing.

VLADIMIR: Let us not waste our time in idle discourse! *(Pause. Vehemently.)* Let us do something, while we have the chance! It is not every day that we are needed. Not indeed that we personally are needed. Others would meet the case equally well, if not better. To all mankind they were addressed, those cries for help still ringing in our ears! But at this place, at this moment of time, all mankind is us, whether we like it or not. Let us make the most of it, before it is too late! Let us represent worthily for once the foul brood to which a cruel fate consigned us! What do you say? It is true that when with folded arms we weigh the pros and cons we are no less a credit to our species. The tiger bounds to the help of his congeners without the least reflexion, or else he slinks away into the depths of the thickets. But that is not the question. What are we doing here, *that* is the question. And we are blessed in this, that we happen to know the answer. Yes, in this immense confusion one thing alone is clear. We are waiting for Godot to come—

The Widow's Blind Date
Israel Horovitz
1981

Scene: the baling-press room at a wastepaper company, Wakefield, Massachusetts

Dramatic
George: a man being confronted by his past, 30

In high school, George and his friends gang-raped Margy in a savage encounter that left her scarred for life. Years later, Margy returns to Wakefield to visit her dying brother, and discovers that George has allowed time to warp his memory of the brutal event. Here, George viciously taunts Margy with the "fact" that she "loved" what he and his friends did to her that night.

GEORGE: You've turned into kinda' a dead fish, Marg… *(To Archie.)* She's kinda turned into a dead fish… *(Smiles.)* Not like the old days, huh? You remember how hot she was in the old days, Arch? *(To Margy.)* You remember how hot you were, Bunny? (…) *(To Margy.)* You ain't in no hoity-toity *Worcester,* or no *Springfield,* or no *Nooo Yahwk,* or no *London, England,* or no *Paris, France*…You're in none of those high-fallootin', hoity-toity, swell places, now, Bunny Palumbo! You're home. *Home!* And when you're home, sis'tah, you are what you are. *(Pauses; angrily.) What you are!! (Pauses.)* Gang-banged at Fisherman's Beach and this one comes up smilin' and beggin' for more… beggin' for more! (…)
No touches! No touches! No touches! *(He punches bale; turns and faces Margy.)* Gangbanged! Gangbanged! The whole God damned Senior Class party and this one is still smilin' and beggin' for more… *(In a rage; throaty, whispered yell.)* Bunny Palumbo, Blind Swede's sistah…Bunny, Bunny, hop, hop, hop, huh? Right, right? *(Full voice.)* Fucks like a what? Answer me! Fucks like a *what? ANSWER ME!* (…)
It's up, it's up! It's already up. *(Moves to Archie in a rage.)* I'll be the one to say what comes up and what doesn't come up! I'll be the one! You get me? *You…get…me?* (…)

Because this girl forgets who she is, that's why. This girl thinks she can come back to town and be new...and she can't...she can't. That ain't the way things are. This girl ain't no Princess Margaret...this is plain Margy...Bunny Palumbo...Blind Swede's no-titted sis'tah...our stuck-up Salutatorian. That's who this girl is! This girl is Bunny, the one who got herself gangbanged, Senior Class beach party, Fisherman's Beach, up Lynn way...
(Smiles. He sings.)

> Lynn, Lynn
> The city of sin;
> You'll never get out,
> But, you'll always get in.

(Moves to Margy.)

> Lynn, Lynn
> The city of sin;
> You'll never get out,
> But, you'll always get in.

(Laughs.) Man, oh man! This is a girl with a *baaaaad reputation,* ain't that right?...Fisherman's Beach, Bunny-Marg...up Lynn way...You remember who went first? You remember? *(Stares at Margy.)* Do you remember? I don't hear an answer...I don't hear an answer...I would like an answer! Do you remember who went first? *Do you remember? Do... you...remember?*